If He's
He'll be Dead in the Morning
Journal of a Somewhat Amusing Outdoor Life

J.C. Dougherty

TALES BEGUN IN DOWAGIAC HAVE A WAY OF NOT ENDING ALL THAT WELL
...herein the exceptions
Dowagiac, Michigan – Tuesday, August 14, 1952

Back then to a seven year old from Jersey the Boston Red Sox were just another bunch of bubble gum card guys. The Sox were one of the first you'd chose to risk at flipping in the hopes of winning better players on better teams. Losers since 1918 they were no where near developing the soft spot in my heart and my head they would eventually carve out.

As a Jersey boy the Mick was my guy and the Yankees were my team. They had won three series in a row and were poised to do it again in '52 and '53. Oblivious to the fact that I would one day share in the seemingly endless pain of Red Sox Nation I proudly worn Mantle's number 7 on my back, which I had luckily pulled in the uniform draw as I suited up for my first Little League game, Keds high tops laced snugly in place.

I got "it" in '52 while on our family summer vacation along the sleepy shores of Indian Lake in Dowagiac, Michigan. "It" was a seven, eight foot or so bamboo fishing pole, pretty much as stiff as the proverbial board and all together too long for a four foot long kid to handle. Attached to the tip were another seven or eight feet of braided line and attached to the end of that was a nasty, pointy ended little number 6 Eagle Claw hook.

Now, mind you, this was no fancy split cane rod. It was a single piece of bamboo au natural; the perfect pole for a

barefoot boy with cheeks of tan and nothing to look forward
to but basking in the long and lazy summer afternoons of my
youth by the lake.

The pole was roughly twice as long as I was tall so it took my
very best seven year old effort to toss the baited line out the
necessary ten feet or so from shore to a place where there
always seemed to be waiting an endless swarm of ravenous
little four to six inch fishies ready to perform piranha-like
moves on my bait.

I picked up quickly on the basics of this new sport, gleefully
impaling unsuspecting garden worms on my shiny new hook
despite their best wiggly protestations. .

A bright red and white wooden stick bobber completed this
Rockwellian picture of a young
boy sporting his newly
acquired implement of
piscatorial destruction. Right
off the bat I mastered the
technique of waiting for said

bobber to be fully submerged before sending my
unsuspecting prey hurtling through the air to an indignant
landing on the lawn behind me. It's amazing that some of
these fish were not turned inside out as a result of their
sudden and undignified extraction from the lake.

This deadly tag-team of bamboo and boy would lead to the
almost legendary early demise of fifty-one bluegills, sunnies
and perch during those languid summer days of '52.

But catching that large batch of pan fishies wasn't the only
high point of the summer. Each one landed provided me with
a fresh opportunity to cram a little more dirt under my

fingernails since each catch seemed to necessitate that I dig another worm. And worm digging turned out to be almost as nifty an outdoor adventure as fishing, one that any self respecting young lad would relish and embrace.

I rudely, and without showing a scintilla of respect for the privacy they should have been enjoying in their earthly abodes, routinely extracted worm after wiggly worm to feed my growing appetite for fishing.

It turned out that the source of my worms was our landlord's own private worm farm. He lived in the house adjacent to the cottage we were renting and had created his own little worm haven alongside his garage. The soil had been painstakingly prepared for its tenants by stoking it with irresistible organic kitchen tidbits.

What I had not realized was that our landlord was also an avid fisherman, for somewhat longer than I had been and had cultivated this little private worm factory for his own use not the use of his tenants.

All week long I dug his worms with relish and with enthusiasm, but without permission. I dug them one worm at a time, running back and forth across the twenty yards or so of lawn that separated our cottage from the lake, driven by my newly acquired zeal for the hunt or more accurately the fish.

For one glorious week it was dig a worm, catch a fish, dig a worm, catch a fish ad infinitum.

And on the final day to cover my tracks, Dad replenished the plot with a couple of boxes of store bought wigglers producing an all's well that ends well result.

The big payoff from this summer fun was that in addition to being hooked on catching bluegills, sunnies and perch I got hooked forever on playing in the great outdoors. Although fishing had become my first love it would soon be followed by my second, hunting.

That tango that I would eventually begin with the upland shooting sports began with bouncing Bb's off squirrels to the frustration of both hunter and hunted.

There was also muskrat trapping, followed not long after by the less well known sport of snatching alligator snapping turtles from a little river near home. We'd extract them from the stream by ill-advisedly grabbing their tails barehanded as they lumbered along the bottom in the clear three or four feet of water that ran through the unassuming Rockaway River, nay the majestic Rockaway River in Denville, New Jersey.

Having seized them by their spiny tails we would hoist them at arms length into the canoe where they would proceed to snort, snarl and generally object to their captivity. Ignoring their protests we would immediately turn our attention to the next one. After that first summer outing in Dowagiac there would be no turning back on a lifetime of outdoor adventure.

Early on, like most beginners my efforts centered on how big or how many fish I caught, likewise later I would be concerned with how many birds I shot or squirrels I trapped.

That was until one particularly frigid night in February of 1956.

I would be turning eleven that April and looked forward to assuming my role as one of the big kids on our Little League team.

In the meantime, however, I was even more excited, along with about a dozen other Boy Scouts to be at Camp Allamuchy on my very first winter overnighter. In addition to camping we were planning to do a little ice fishing. This would be a real outdoors-boy tour de force. Allamuchy, hallowed grounds of my childhood summer camp experiences was, and presumably still is a pristine nature reserve consisting of 997 acres tucked away in a quiet corner of Stanhope, New Jersey.

Scout troops and scouts during the 50's typically outfitted themselves with an array of WWII army surplus stuff; tents, sleeping bags, utensils, canteens, cookware, latrine shovels... you name it. Troop 118 was no different.

The trouble with surplus equipment, however was that our fighting boys in Europe had been pretty rough on their gear so by the time it trickled down to the Rockaway Army & Navy Surplus Store it was not unusual for most of the old sidewall tents we bought to be missing half or more of their tent peg tie-downs. Tie-downs are the little tabs that allowed the tent sides to be anchored by pegs to the ground.

These sidewall tents consisted of a ridge pole supported by two vertical poles at each end and, unlike modern tents did not have floors. This permitted the side walls, if not securely anchored with pegs, to flap in the slightest breeze.

My tent-mate, best friend and snapping turtle hunting companion extraordinaire, Andy and I were both newbies to scouting. Andy was Opie right out of central casting. He was the original frog-in-the-pocket kid with jeans sporting ripped out knees years before it become fashionable.

Our status as newbies meant that we got the last pick of available tents that weekend and therefore it should not have come as a surprise that ours had only two of its original eight tie-downs intact. The default solution to this problem was to drive a tent peg right through the body of the tent canvass to anchor the walls. It was, however, February and this proved to be an unworkable strategy since the ground was frozen solid.

Rocks then, strategically placed would be our fall-back position. Trouble was most of the rocks around our campsite were also frozen to the ground. We seemed to be running out of strategies.

The hike to the campsite in question had taken over an hour from our arrival at Allamuchy base camp but only later did we find out that the trail we'd trudged for that hour to get to the site was really just a giant loop so that we were in reality only about two hundred yards from were we began.

This would allow a hasty retreat to the scout masters vehicle in the event of some outdoorsy mishaps. The scout masters however had not shared this information with us, as they knew we would have groused endlessly about this long and unnecessary character-building stroll through the winter woods.

Notwithstanding our peg tab-less ten Andy and I after a struggle managed to set up the tent by tying tether lines to nearby trees and by scavenging up what rocks we were able to dislodge from the frozen earth. Tent erected we could at last settle into the comfort provided by a roaring campfire and our first campfire cooked meal… ya know the traditional scout menu consisting of hot dogs on sticks, cold Vienna sausage and beans a là can.

The ground was too frozen to get into a game of mumbley peg, one of our favorite camping pastimes. You know mumbley-peg, the game where you toss a pocketknife into the ground in a progressively more difficult array of competitive tricks.

If the knife tossed by a player does not stick in the bare ground, the player loses his/her turn.

"Tip of the fingers" was one trick with the knife being required to stick in the ground after doing a somersault off the tip of each index finger. Next was "Tony Chestnut" where the knife was similarly flipped off the toe, the knee, the chest and the forehead (nut). The rules provided that the knife had to stick into the ground upright enough to allow a challenger to put two fingers under it. But I digress...

It turned out to be an attention-riveting cold that night and even with an assist from that roaring campfire so we all turned in early. Camping equates to fit-full sleep even in nice weather, and little protection was afforded by the Army issue sleeping bags that were made of 100% wool and referred to as mummy sacks. This deathly metaphor should have been sufficient to drive me toward selecting another form of bedding but the price was right. Mummy sacks were scratchy bedding with not-so-water-proof shells into which the wool sack became a liner supposedly designed to protect from the weather.

Imagine lying outdoors in sub-freezing temps wrapped in one wool blanket.

So it was not surprising that with the arrival of daybreak I awoke to a missing tent-mate. Andy was nowhere to be seen and I supposed that he had been as cold as I and had high

tailed back to the main campfire that our scout masters no
doubt would have already coaxed into a roaring blaze. Odd
that Andy was nowhere to be seen and odder still that the
inside of our tent was so white.

And why was the tip of my nose both cold and wet?

Slowly dawning on me was the fact that Andy was missing
only because unlike me he was still in the tent.

It had snowed that night, an inch or two and there were still a
few flakes dancing around in the morning breeze. Those few
had joined the others that had lightly dusted every inch of my
mummy sack during the night.

I had become a five foot long white lump, prone alongside
our tent completely covered with snow. Since our tent
lacked the necessary tie downs to secure its sides, I had
managed at some point to roll out of the tent under the
unsecured sidewall only to be blanketed by the white stuff.

Turned out I was just fine, no colder outside than I would
have been inside, so we got on with our planned morning of
ice fishing followed by a lunch of more Vienna Sausages.

The idea was to break camp in the afternoon and head back
since we still faced (we thought) the same hour out hike as
we'd encountered hiking in.

So, being good scouts determined to leave the place better
than we found it, we patrolled the area for debris of any kind,
bagging it in two large garbage bags before falling in around
2pm for our return hike.

The scout master first asked for a volunteer to carry the garbage out since, as he said, "It won't walk out on its own", and predictably Buddy Tilson raised his hand. Questionable judgment at best, Buddy.

We began the hike out but within the first fifty yards were told that we would not be taking the left trail at the fork near camp that would have had us retrace our original path in, but the right trail instead. It was then that we were told that we had been taken in the long way (the character building route), and that the alternative way out was considerably shorter. This route was about the distance of two football fields and would bring our little troop back to the base camp in a matter of minutes.

The trouble was that Buddy had lingered briefly to repack and consolidate the garbage so that, lagging behind by a mere two or three minutes when he attempted to catch up with the rest of the group he had no idea that in fact he shouldn't take the original trail out.

So he did. Six hours later a gaggle of state troopers found Buddy in the pitch black out on the highway, still carrying the garbage bags trying to hitchhike his way back.

What's memorable about this little ice fishing/camping excursion was not the couple of bass we managed to catch that day, but the memories of a snow covered Jim and Wandering Buddy the consummate "leave it cleaner than you found it" scout.

Long after bagging a limettè (one bird or fish short of a limit is technically a limettè) and once the images of landing the big one have faded, I re-live these little adventures most enjoyably by revisiting the funny stuff, the odd, unexpected things that made each trip unique.

Don't get me wrong, catching a lunker or dropping a pa'tridge with a dead on right-to-left crossing shot still has its merits but there's nothing like the occasional miscue to make it all the more interesting.

When I reminisce with friends the stories we tell each other only infrequently have anything to do with the size of the trout or the number of woodcock or pheasant... they more often have to do with the embarrassing missed shots and stream filled waders. Our best times are peppered with the little indignities that accompany getting to play in the big outdoors just like we did when we were young.

Andy and I lost touch after high school, but I was fortunate to find a new crew to hang with. I have yet to arise and find any of them asleep in the snow, but I'm pretty sure it's only a matter of time.

THE NEW CREW

Once I hit New England I fell in with a new crew. There were really two new crews. One, the group of guys who shared my love of hunting and fishing, another who made their living playing baseball at Fenway Park. One made me laugh while the other often made me weep.

Jack, cross my heart and hope to die, is, like me another Jersey boy who was able to escape the Garden State under cover of darkness. Our 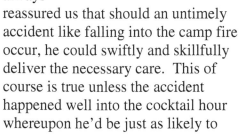resident cow doctor, his medical training always reassured us that should an untimely accident like falling into the camp fire occur, he could swiftly and skillfully deliver the necessary care. This of course is true unless the accident happened well into the cocktail hour whereupon he'd be just as likely to recommend declawing.

Hank, better known to his close friends as the Mad Hatter, is the MacGyver every group needs to have along in the event they find themselves stranded on the proverbial desert island or more germane to our group, adrift without paddle or power on the Merrimack River headed out to sea.

Bennie the Bean Counter, also from Jersey was elected by acclamation to the unpaid positions of both treasurer and recording secretary of our little group based solely on the fact that at our first organizational meeting he was the only one who brought a pen. Not a skilled outdoorsman, Ben was always willing to learn and was a heck of a card player.

Willie, believe it or not is another transplant from New Jersey. He made a career out of accumulating funny stories and combined that with a knock for telling them. So, naturally sales was his game… but he was smart enough to know that it was hunting and fishing that really mattered.

JC is, of course, yours truly. Born a Georgia peach I've been moving northward all my life despite the increasingly cold weather that I've encountered. I grew up mostly in New Jersey, alien land to Dixie boys like me, with one foot in a stream and the other on a ball field. To my delight I discovered early on that fishing is much funnier than baseball.

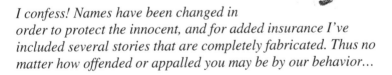

I confess! Names have been changed in order to protect the innocent, and for added insurance I've included several stories that are completely fabricated. Thus no matter how offended or appalled you may be by our behavior…

This, in the words of my attorney, will give you and all your friends the cover of "plausible deniability".

HOWARD'S PLACE
West Kennebec, Maine – Saturday, October 4, 1975

It was a bright morning with temps in the mid 60's. It was also opening day of the woodcock season which happened to fall on the first Saturday in October this year. The Red Sox, their opening day now only a distant memory were, scheduled to be in a playoff against the Oakland A's that Saturday

It looked promising for the local nine since Oakland would be missing the services of ace hurler Catfish Hunter. Boston manager Darrell Johnson entrusted both the ball and the mound to el Tiante and he obliged by throwing a beauty.

The A's managed just 3 hits to the delight of the Fenway faithful that day. Life was good.

'75 was also the year the torch was to be passed from the fading champs of the 1967 season to the new kids. Yaz, Petrocelli and Tony C. were still there but had been reshuffled to make room for Burleson, Pudge Fisk and a couple of outfield additions. Dwight, aka "the arm", Evans had become our resident right fielder during the two previous seasons and was about to be joined by Jim Rice and Fred Lynn, in left and center respectively.

Lynn snagged both the MVP and Rookie of the Year awards with a .331 average along with 21 homers.

Rice posted outstanding numbers even though he didn't make it to the field until June and ended the season on the DL with a hand broken by the errant toss of am opposing pitcher. Still, in his shortened season he averaged .309, drove in 102 runs and walloped 22 home runs. This, we thought, would be the season, both woodcock and baseball to end all seasons.

So many memories revolve around a discussion of shots taken, shots missed, fish hooked, fish missed and the Red Sox.

...We went hunting.

I spent the better part of fifteen years, give or take, hunting the nooks, crannies and fields behind Howard's place. To this day I remember it as the finest cover for upland hunting that I've ever encountered. And until the very last day I hunted there, our little band of four, sometimes five weekend shooters always had the place exclusively to ourselves. For some reason we never quite understood, the owner never seemed to let anyone else hunt the farm.

Eventually after Howard was gone things changed a little. His son, Carl opened the farm up to anyone asking permission. So the last time I went there we bumped into a couple of other hunters. That marked the end of an era. I never went back.

Not that it was exactly crowded there; plenty of elbow room. The farm was an upland shooters paradise. My best guess is that it was the better part of two hundred acres, maybe more, maybe less. I must admit, if you're looking for someone to guess the number of jellybeans in a big jar, look somewhere else. I'm not very good at that sort of thing. Anyway it was big, a bunch of acres of the best bird cover imaginable. I get positively giddy when I think about it.

Most of the covers were bordered by gently neglected pastures where young aspen and maples were cautiously beginning to stage a come back. Most fields were rimmed by alder swales on one side or another, a favorite of our little friend the wily woodcock. But then the whole farm was really just one big cover.

Almost everywhere we were surrounded by a canopy of second growth forest that hid the skeletal remains of ancient orchards and what used to be open pasture. The orchards were beaten and neglected, but were still working hard at their assigned task of bearing fruit

Roughly assembled rock walls were also everywhere, frequently surrounded by the returning woods as the farm activity had slowly diminished over the years and the once-groomed pastures they bordered were no longer being maintained.

The rock walls were a silent but constant and sturdy reminder of the harsh beginnings that New England settlers must have faced as they knuckled down to eke a living out of this rugged land. Before you could plant one potato (pronounced "ba-day-doh" in Maine) it was generally necessary to move at least two rocks.

When we first started hunting in West Kennebunk Howard's place was still a working farm though clearly not all that hard working. Howard was more than a hand full of years past his 70th birthday when we met him. His aforementioned son, Carl along with grandson Carl Jr. lived across the street. They were clearly busy with lives of their own so helping around the farm was at best a catch as catch activity for them.

The farm still had a few pastures that were kept trimmed haphazardly by a handful of grazing cows and a few swaybacks that thankfully roamed around indifferent to our bird hunting intrusions.

The first time we met, or more accurately were confronted by Howard, was just a couple of weekends after we had stealthily hunted his farm for the first time. We were returning one early Saturday morning in October for another go at it. It was the bird season of '75.

Since we hadn't bothered to ask permission to hunt the farm
we were careful to park a healthy distance from house we
assumed belonged to the owner. We could see the old
colonial which was an easy hundred yards from where we
parked. The house was perched imposingly on a knoll it
shared with a gnarly but stately ancient maple. Since we
clearly knew it housed the owner of the farm, making the
excuse that we didn't know who to ask for permission really
didn't wash.

Of course we had convinced ourselves that the home was
probably not that of the owner of the property we were about
to hunt on, reluctant as we were to ask permission for fear if
would not be given. Instead, we would rely on a comically
obvious approach, one that easily exposed our trespassing
ways to the bright light of day; we simply parked down the
road a bit, all in order to try to maintain our access. Sneaky,
we thought, was our middle name.

So that October morning our band of four had parked, pulled
out our gear to a chorus of yelping, whining dogs and were
setting about dropping some field load sevens and ?eights
into our small arsenal of 20 gauge shotguns as we prepared to
walk the fence line to the out-back fields and alder stands.
Then he appeared.

Without, as they say any warning, as if emerging suddenly
from under a steaming cow hod there was Howard. He came
charging across the open field that separated his house from
our parking spot, waving a pair of hands the size of catchers'
mitts over his head. He came through the winter rye on boots
big enough to make crop circles. To say he was skinny as a
rail would be to accuse rails of anorexia. He got to us
quicker than green corn goes through the new maid.

18

An agitated sight to behold, it's hard to recall what it was about this animated, crusty old dervish that stood out but I distinctly remember his hat. It was a baseball cap, mesmerizing, a study in how austere Yankees are always able to wring every ounce of utility out of all their possessions, especially objects of clothing.

It was clear that this cap had served its' wearer well. It didn't owe him a nickel as it had seen him through winter chill, spring rains and blistering summer heat. It was also clear that it had been his constant companion through every chore imaginable at the farm from chicken feeding time to tractor repair. It had even held its ground against his sweaty brow even when he was putting up the ten or so obligatory cords of wood each fall that would be necessary to heat the old colonial.

It was a cap from which you could likely have wrung a quart of motor oil, the brim delaminating and starting to resemble the bill of a duck. Yet you could still make out the faded, faint remains of "Dodd's Feed & Grain" embroidered above the brim. At least it looked like it might once have been the word "Dodd's"... it could actually have been "Saskatchewan" for all I know.

By any account it was a cap to be reckoned with. It was the cap to end all caps, destined to be enshrined in all likelihood in the Maine Cap Hall of Fame up to Augusta but for the fierce competition in the annual "best of cap" run off in the person of, and in the cap of Lloyd "The Hat" Bickford of Unity... but that's another story.

To their credit and my amazement Jack and Willie were able to screw up enough courage to intercept Howard about fifteen strides from where The Mad Hatter and I now stood motionless.

Without hesitation but with uncanny instinct both Jack and Willie immediately assumed the hunkering position, a move that induced Howard involuntarily to do the same.
Hunkering is that well known, down home posture that little kids take naturally, but that older knees find painful.

Hunkering, for the uninitiated among you, is that traditional country pose which, when assumed, is both disarming while at the same time suggesting sincerity, honesty and a certain "get down to business" attitude among fellow hunkerers.

These would prove to be handy nonverbal messages given our trespassing ways.

After an initial opening statement, punctuated by flailing hands, still hunkered Howard grabbed a nearby stick and began scratching in the dirt. He seemed to be drawing something but if so remained focused on delivering his message to Jack and Willie. It's a well know fact that dirt drawing and hunkering go hand in hand even if what you're drawing has nothing to do with the conversation.

Still at a safe distance, I had been preoccupied with keeping a couple of overly ready-to-go dogs corralled. This was enough distraction that I was unable to make out what the three of them were talking about. I just figured that since

Howard hadn't thrown us off his property... yet... it was a good thing. We were all very fond of good things.

Eventually the hunkering ended and six knees creaking, all three got up. With a decisive adjustment to the brim(s) of his hat, Howard abruptly turned and headed back across the field toward the house.

Jack and Willie came back grins already firmly in position. "Well that went well", said Jack. "He told us we can hunt here anytime we like. He just wants us to park up in the driveway at his house so if he hears some shooting he'll know we're out back."

"Wh, wh, what did you say to him?" I said.

"Not much", he Jack said. "He just wanted to know if I was the veterinarian."

Thusly, was forever cast in stone, the First Axiom of Upland Hunting, befriend a veterinarian as your hunting companion.

There's nothing handier when trekking through rural New Hampshire or Maine than to have along someone who actually speaks the language. Another theory has it that cow doctors seem to also exude an implicit promise of gratuitous services or at a minimum other valuable cow and horse fixing advice. This of course goes a long way when coaxing permission to hunt or other necessary information from the likes of most of the chronically distrustful farmers you're likely to encounter.

In this case it seems the back of Jack's Suburban "hunt mobile" had been examined by Howard on our earlier visit while we were out back hunting. Howard apparently saw and recognized the evidence that was the clutter of Jack's tools of his veterinarian trade scattered about the back of the truck.

It was a pretty simple deduction for Howard to have put that particular two and the other two together... cow doctor.

Thereafter having secured carte blanche permission to hunt Howard's place, each fall, come opening day, we would pile into whatever the then current hunt mobile was and trundle up the Maine pike to West Kennebunk.

There was, of course, the obligatory stop for a sub and soda which got tucked into game pouches in anticipation of the traditional lunch break on Lunch Break Knoll. Lunch Break Knoll was a grassy clearing, invariably dusted by a few of the first fallen leaves of the season where we somehow always seemed to arrive around the noon hour. It was consistently a sunny little spot where we could refresh, replenishing body and soul, while recounting the mornings hunt, points, retrieves, bird count and other relevant activities.

But I had been telling you about opening days. Normally on arrival we would pull up to the farm house silently holding our breath wondering if Howard had survived another always harsh Maine winter, unpredictable spring and unbearably hot summer. We looked forward to the fifteen minutes or so with Howard wherein he would fill us in on the hunting conditions we might expect, along with other important topics mostly having to do with the weather.

"Lots of woodcock out back" he would occasionally inform us in a voice that sounded like he was trying to woo a wood rasp. "I saw one yesterday was so big it was standing flatfooted mating a coon."

Ah, Maine.

Several years into our relationship with Howard, on one unusually warm October opening day, we pulled up to the house near the screened kitchen door, windows fully down to capture what little breeze was around.

From inside a familiar, high pitched voice could be heard bellowing, "The boys are here, the boys are here!" Talk about music to our ears. Once again Howard was alive, well and our access to this private hunting paradise assured for another season.

More significantly we seem to have been quietly, unceremoniously elevated to some sort of familial status. We were "the boys". High praise indeed! Higher praise was in store. Unprompted after exchanging the usual pleasantries, Howard asked if we would mind writing down our names and addresses.

Hum... You can imagine the speculation that tore through our ranks as to why. "He probably wants to put us in his will granting access to the land in perpetuity!" "Maybe he wants to send us the Burnside family Christmas letter".

Never did find out.

But it was enough to know that we had become family... or at least he always made us feel that way. Periodically, we'd return from a day's hunt to find a few prize-winning Blue Hubbard squash neatly tucked into the back of our SUV's. That sort of thing tends to happen when you previously have mentioned that you've found that a roasted Blue Hubbard drenched in brown sugar is the perfect compliment to roasted Partridge.

WHY WOODOCK?

You may wonder why we invested so much energy in the pursuit of this little bird that so many have never even heard of.

I agree. It bears a little explanation.

The woodcock is a diminutive, shadowy little critter common to New England and other gentile uplands where the landscapes are typically framed by indigenous aspen and alder thickets. It is not uncommon for these woodcock sanctuaries to be found adjacent to peaceful little streams bordered by boot sticky muck.

The woodcock has been highly regarded and sought after by passionate, irrational members of a small cult of upland hunters who annually travel the back woods of New England in search this elusive little bird. Woodcock are also a catalyst triggering the gathering of these small groups for the corollary purpose of imbibing the fermented grains from less familiar regions, frequently Tennessee.

It is not uncommon in these gatherings that typically surround woodstoves or other friendly hearths for woodcock hunters to be accompanied by companions well schooled in the art of barking.

I still remember the first time I saw and shot at a woodcock. That woodcock no doubt still remembers it too and chuckles at the thought.

They are like pleasant little winged gypsies. They move silently at night and, rumor has it, frequently kidnap the children of hunter's souls. The lore and legend surrounding them have spawned dozens of nicknames, always descriptive, always affectionate including wood snipes, little twisters, bog suckers, pop eyes, swamp partridges, mud snipes and the perennial favorite Timberdoodle.

Hunters generally believe that flight birds arrive in groups but the reality is that these little creatures are very individualistic.

Every upland hunter derives more than just the obvious pleasures that come with spending countless hours afield in search of the wary woodcock. among those the sights, sounds and smells of fall. The crisp sound of autumn leaves crackling under foot and there's the special whiff of wet dog as they scamper by in search of game oblivious to your every command.

EGG OF WOODCOCK

It is inevitable therefore that hunting woodcock naturally begs the eternal question… which came first, the woodcock or the egg?

FIFTEEN MINUTES OF FAME AT FENWAY
Fenway Park, Boston, MA – October 21, 1975

We had swept the A's and finished first in the East with a record of 95 wins and 65 losses. But the real highlight of the season began with a sweep of the Twins in Minnesota followed by another sweep in Texas.

At the All-Star break the Sox had a 4.5 game lead over the Yankees and Brewers. They then won 10 in a row moving 6 in front of the Bombers before putting them away for good taking 3 out of 4 in New York.

Then… we began holding our collective breaths for the post season.

Normally, there are not a whole lot of things that would keep me out of the field or off the stream, but Bobby T., childhood friend, erstwhile first baseman and teammate on the Denville Rotary Little League team, had scored a couple of box seats for the big game at Fenway.

It was the sixth game of the World Series.

I know that it's probably closing in on a couple of million fans who claim to have been at that game. Trust me… I was there! Watch the films! That's me in the first row, left field side with my right elbow perched on the camera well next to the Cincinnati dugout, the not then quite so notorious Pete Rose no more than thirty feet directly in front of me holding down third.

I did not go hunting that Tuesday.

Carlton Fisk was never better, nor will he ever be better remembered for any moment in his 24 year career than for The Home Run!

Never mind catching 2,226 games or being an 11-time All-Star. It was in Game 6 of the 1975 World Series facing Cincinnati Reds pitcher Pat Darcy when he hit a pitch down the left field line toward the foul pole. It hit the pole not in small part due to Fisk willing it toward fair ground with the now classic wave of his arms as he trotted sideways up the first base line.

So I became a part, a very brief part of the landscape of Red Sox history. Not exactly the fifteen minutes of fame as advertised but forever fully emerged in that historic moment. There are shots of the Cincinnati dugout that clearly show yours truly in attendance.

The big game that Tuesday sucked all the air out of thoughts of Howard's place and the approaching end of the woodcock season. Never mind that the deer season was a short week and a half away and that its' opening traditionally marked the end of bird season in Maine. Sharing a bird cover with a deer hunters was never a good idea.

So it was a big deal that on that particular, sunny, utterly pleasant October afternoon in anticipation of the Big Red Machine making another appearance at Fenway Park I did not go hunting.

I'm still not able to discuss game seven.

TRIALS, TRIBULATIONS AND BLACK FLIES ON THE OSSIPEE
Center Ossipee, New Hampshire – May 6, 7, 8, 1976

Way to go guys! Some follow up to the '75 season. Third place? Really?

This was also the year A's owner Charlie Finley tried to palm off Joe Rudi and Rollie Fingers to the Sox for $1 million each. Sorry Charlie.

This was also the year Bill "Spaceman" Lee pitching at Yankee Stadium was injured when in defending his teams honor over a collision between Lou Pinella and Pudge Fisk wound up in a heap. Said heap was created when Graig Nettles slammed him to the ground in the ensuring scuffle.

This was also the year Wade Boggs was drafted in the seventh round.
This was also the year of Tom Yawkey's demise.

This was also the year Don Zimmer (aka Elmer Fudd) took the reigns from Darrell Johnson.

Bit of trivia: It was in fact Red Sox Nation that coined the phrase "Oh well, wait until next year".

Our years of hunting and fishing trips were launched with a long May weekend combo camping and brook trout excursion to the Ossipee River in West Ossipee, New Hampshire in '76.

This first trip had been hyped well in advance of the event by the telling and retelling of grandiose tales of the great, nay legendary trout that could be taken from the Ossipee... tales spun by Hank.

Trips to the Ossipee had been the stuff of Hanks childhood, a place where he had fished and frolicked in pre- and post-pubescent bliss. It should be pointed out that a six inch trout in the hands of a ten year old appears to be substantially larger than that same trout held up for a snapshot and a smile by a middle aged adult.

What did the rest of us know? There wasn't a single native New Englander among us, save Hank. We bought his large trout tales hook, line and, well you know.

None of us knew anything about trout fishing in New England. As an accident of my birth in Georgia, my somewhat limited areas of expertise were confined to the subjects of pecans, peaches and Vidalia onions. The other three guys were about as much help, all sporting New Jersey roots, of little practical help in the great north woods of New England where waders with pointy toes were not in style. When it came to finding fishing spots in our newly adopted homeland we were pretty much at The Mad Hatter's mercy, a mercy you don't particularly want to be at. (With apologies for the previous sentence to my high school sophomore English teacher Miss Sullivan)

Trusting souls as we then were, freshly immersed in new friendships we assembled our rag-tag band of starry-eyed, greenhorn fishermen at the Park Lunch for a planning session for this our first outing.

The Park Lunch is plain, not fancy catering to the pizza and beer crowd; no quiche allowed. We quickly adopted the "Lunch" as our traditional annual meeting, planning and daydreaming spot.

As a high school math teacher and therefore I guess presumed to be quick with things arithmetic Ben became the de facto recording secretary of the group scrawling notes on napkins and coasters in order to immortalize our list of gear and goods. His skill adding up a column of grocery charges quickly earned him the moniker Benny the Bean Counter. Come to think of it we never knew if he was actually any good at it. Took him at his word, being too lazy to check his work.

Our first order of business as we gathered that first evening was to resolve that there would be no bending on the "No Girls Allowed" rule. You know, the same rule that every barefoot boy posted on their newly erected clubhouse/tree house door. With good reason we chortled and agreed as we ticked off the myriad of reasons why not.

29

"Fish don't compare you to other fishermen and don't expect you to still be friends after you release them. They also don't care if you fall asleep in the middle of catching them." said Hank.

"Do these waders make my butt look big?" chimed in Jack followed by "Should I wear the Orvis vest or the lower cut Bean vest?"

"You're crazy if you think I'm going out on the river now. I can't do a thing with my hair!" said Ben.

Willie finished up with "There's no way we'll end up playing charades instead of poker around the campfire."

I added that on a fishing trip no one is permitted to be judgmental; at least no one who expects to get invited a second time.

The business portion of the meeting behind us we proceeded to plan for the trip.

Community stuff like tents and camp kitchen utensils were always the first order of business and early on the trend was toward individual accommodations, or at best, two man tents.

At the top of the gear list each year was "The Skillet". The Skillet was of the three leg cast iron variety, the kind that would sit comfortably over a campfire's bed of coals, ready and eager to receive a bunch of sunny side overs or a pile of hash browns. For that matter the Skillet was capable of holding both at the same time along with a gaggle of brook trout and a pound of bacon.

It was massive, a full 16 inches or so in diameter. For the disbelievers I offer actual photographic evidence although this candid shows only a bevy of sizzling brookies.

A discussion of our camp breakfast however, is premature. First, we had to get ourselves to this little slice of paradise called the Ossipee...and have breakfast along the way.

So in early May we went about getting there.

This first trip to Ossipee began inauspiciously with a stop for breakfast about half way up on old Route 16. The spot we chose was an all purpose establishment where, in addition to breakfast one could obtain gas, fishing lures, Slim Jims, a refrigerator magnet in the shape of the Granite State and by the way if the spirit moved you, you could both buy and mail a post card to your grammy.

The six of us scrunched up in a booth and after a short wait a not so comely waitress straight from central casting wandered over and plunked a freshly filled ketchup bottle on the table. She was underweight, with a wire-y build and I imagined had quick cat-like movements should the occasion call for it.

No, sorry I'm thinking of someone else...

Our waitress asked, "You guys ready to order?"

We were.

I'll spare you the details of who went the over easy route... who went sunny side up and on which platters the sausages or bacon were expected to go. Point is all went smoothly until it was Hank's turn.

"A couple of scrambled, bacon, white toast" he said.

That seemed a straightforward enough order.

"How would you like them scrambled?" she asked.

A confused silence swept over the booth.

She of course meant, do you want them scrambled soft as in runny or hard as in... hard.

We of course had no idea what she meant.

Whereupon Hank picked up his fork and began to make that familiar rapid, little circular motion you associate with actually scrambling eggs in a bowl. "Like this" he offered, still not understanding why a breakfast establishment in semi-rural New Hampshire would not know how to scramble an egg.

And so with that the first of many fishing and hunting adventures by our little group to the North Country began.

Laden with gear, grocery shopping done, coolers packed with ice and other outdoorsy sundries our SUV caravan continued up Route 16 on our way to West Ossipee where we would hang a left and head up the little mountain road to the campsite.

The ride to Ossipee back in '76 was a bit like I would imagine any self respecting sci-fi time traveler might experience. It didn't seem like '76, more like '56.

It was rural New Hampshire at it's picturesque best straight out of an earlier era; roadside establishments with dysfunctional neon signs proclaiming "EATS", old timey Esso gas stations, homes cleverly disguised as shanties with the obligatory lifetime collection of defunct washing machines and unregistered vehicles neatly displayed on their lawns.

A high point of the scenery that year was one such modest abode displaying a large roughly hand painted sign which read: "Wife wanted. Must be able to cook, clean and have own truck. Send picture of truck"

Our guide, The Mad Hatter, led the way up the mountain to the campsite with his usual flourish, pulling in and insisting on a spot which looked, truth be told, pretty uninteresting.

Yet we pressed on, setting up camp with the first order of business tent pitching. I had a pup, newly acquired for cross country travel. But after Susan and I made our initial trip we had quickly determined that Kampgrounds of America needed to yield to cheap but more comfortable motels. Consequently the pup was in "as new" condition having been used just one time.

Job two was rock gathering. A proper cooking/campfire pit required gathering a thoughtful selection of rocks in order to construct an edifice worthy of the culinary masterpieces we anticipated preparing. We put Ben and Willie in charge on the theory that between them their Italian ancestry would show them the way.

Campfire edifice built, we finally we hit the stream around 11 am with plans to reconnect at 2 for lunch so we could compare fishy notes and lie to each other about the big ones that got away.

After nearly three hours of flailing the water, my little section of the stream had produced nothing but brookies in the 3 to 4 inch range. This was actually fine since my attention was of necessity actually focused more on the swarms of black flies which felt like they were also of the 3 to 4 inch variety.

It seemed I was a veritable mosquito and black fly magnet. The cruel joke eventually became that I was only invited along to attract the pesky little creatures to me instead of to them. …or was it a joke?

Being the slow learner that I was it took several more trips to Ossipee until I realized that the black fly problem had its' roots in my attire, not my physiology. I had purchased a snappy leather hat in New York just prior to our escape to the country and my fashion conscience self knew it would just be the bee's knees to compliment my also snappy fishing attire.

Trouble was the lingering natural scent of bovine body oils still present in the leather proved to be an irresistible attractor for both black flies and mosquitoes. By the time I finished up the morning fishing excursion and headed back to camp, I had developed a 360 degree welt about a ¼ inch thick and two inches wide just below the hat brim where the biting beasties had managed to encircle my head. The swelling had caused my ears to become the cauliflower ears of a seasoned boxer.

Bugs aside, Ben, Jack, Willie and I got back to camp just before Hank and had already broken out the Oreos and hot Italian peppers as a pre lunch snack-a-tizer. We were washing down the yummies with a few beers and commiserating over the poor trout showing since mini brookies seemed to be the order of the day for all of us.

Then Hank strolled in beaming. "Hey. How'd you guys do?" he said.

"Metz a Metz" we shrugged and chimed in unison. "You?"

"Unbelievable" he said. "Got my limit and then some" the actual meaning of limit being of little practical concern to Hank.

At which point he reached into his breast pocket and produced a small Glad Sandwich Bag, which was doing double duty that day as a creel and which appeared to be full of close cousins of the 3 to 4 inch discards the rest of us had caught and released that morning. In fact the entire weekend produced only one trout that was over four inches.

Jack won the pool with a brook trout of the commanding size of five and three-quarter inches. His catch so impressed us that we insisted he show us the exact spot where he landed such a prize. So close on his heels, we beat through the underbrush for five or ten sweaty minutes alongside a trickle of a stream that no where along its run exceeded even a foot in depth.

At last we stood gawking in awe at a rock about 10 inches in diameter behind which the luckless brookie had been feeding. So much for the legendary trout of the mighty Ossipee land of Hank's youth.

Adding insult to injury, the black flies were relentless, having thrown their lot in with their mosquito brethren in an all out attack which lasted well into sundown and beyond. No amount of bug juice, no amount of mosquito netting, no amount of silent prayer can provide sufficient deterrence to their determined onslaught. They are especially adept at squeezing under even the most tightly fitted shirt cuff or stealthily sneaking under the brim of your snuggest fishing hat.

Eventually my defense of last resort was to re-pitch my tent about three feet from the campfire and sit inside it each night with the mosquito netting zipped up. That way I could still be part of the evening's festivities but remain protected from the relentless attacks by the black flies and mosquitoes.

These little extended weekend trips up north in search of brook trout were never very expensive. On the other hand, on many occasions we'd return with very little in the way of trout bagged to show for our efforts. Once, musing over our lack of success, I mentioned that on that particular trip I had calculated given my outlay for the trip that the single trout I caught had cost me about $50.

It was then pointed out to me that it was probably therefore a good thing then I had only caught one which kept the trip quite affordable.

GAMEY VITTLES AND OTHER CULINARY DELIGHTS
Durham, New Hampshire – February 19, 1976

With the 1975 season behind us we spent the winter looking forward to spring training and the promise of greatness on the heels of Fisk's walk-off homer in game six.

Ho-hum! '76 would not be a repeat of other disappointing years unless by repeat you mean the endless parade of "also ran" years we'd become so accustomed to. Nothing went well. Bowie Kuhn wouldn't let them trade for Rollie Fingers and Joe Rudi. Jean Yawkey, in a stroke of baseball brilliance, replaced Darrell Johnson with the Fudd Man (Don Zimmer).

Ho-hum!

Food always played a central role in our little excursions. Get up… breakfast, usually at one of Maine's countless breakfast counters… hunt… break for lunch over liverwurst with slabs of red onion and spicy mustard on rye… hunt 'til dusk… snackatizer… self lubricate with loud mouth soup (martinis or bourbon)… dinner, bed and repeat. This is a simple formula but one that served us well and has stood the test of time.

One of our first meals on many of these trips was turkey with all the trimmings, the remains of which contributed to our last meal of the trip... our own version of a thousand year old soup compressed into seven days. At one of the spots where we stayed into the pot on the old Glenwood stove went scraps from every meal during resulting by the end of the week in a rich, thick soupy brew that was never the same twice yet each year was proclaimed to be the best yet.

There were other culinary delights, like the Ritz Cracker mock apple pie desert the "mock" of which wasn't at all necessary since we'd invariably had just spent a full day walking through vintage, deserted overflowing apple orchards in search of the ever wary partridge.

My personal favorite was the generic "snackatizer" which described any muchie within arms length at the end of the day.

Our Annual Game Dinner was the social zenith of the year. Invitations were dolled out sparingly, planning was a gargantuan task, selection of the location critical, cooking assignments were carefully doled out.

Our biggest challenge was keeping a straight face when sampling each other's woodcock dishes. Woodcock for the uninitiated isn't just a dark gamy meat it's a very dark, very gamey meat, the consistency of liver with little to recommend it.

Traditional preparations include the most trusted recipe of all. Skillet Doodle which involved breasting the birds, thereby averting the dreaded plucking ritual then marinating said breasts overnight in a zesty blend of orange juice, red curry and cooking sherry. Thusly prepped the breasts then were dredged in cornmeal and deep fried in a cast iron skillet.

Unfortunately, even this preparation usually fails to mask the strong flavor and as that old joke goes, the better alternative would be throwing out the bird and eating the skillet.

One year we went overboard providing oysters, little neck clams and an obscene array of other appetizers at home number one followed by a bus ride to the five course game dinner at home number two. Providing a bus for invitees was a particularly good idea, at least for me given my past experiences combining vehicular operation with consumption of brown stuff.

I recall one evening when my designated wife and driver was out of town visiting her sister and I found myself at a gathering where, in addition to brown stuff, recreational everything else was making the rounds. Almost immediately the munchies beset me so I parked myself quite strategically near a platter of deviled eggs. Trouble was upon consumption of three or four eggs a little paranoia set in and I readily convinced myself that everyone at the party was talking about my unseemly egg behavior.

It was at that point that I determined a hasty exit was the only solution and I beat a path back to my car. In addition to rampant paranoia most of my critical motor skills had become a tad fuzzy and as I proceeded to make my way home (down as remote a route as possible) it became clear that I shouldn't be driving. Try telling that to a drunk! My main problem was that in addition to my condition, a little fog had settled in.

So I was able only to drive twenty or thirty yards at a time. I would then stop the car, get out, walk ahead to check out the road, get back in drive another twenty or thirty yards then repeat. This was only necessary for a distance of about a quarter mile until the fog lifted but I now refer to it as the evening I had to walk my car home.

Back to the year of the bus trip which produced the now infamous quote: "After I finish running through these slides you guys would probably enjoy seeing the ones of our family trip to Yellowstone."

Now kids don't try this at home. This is strictly for professionals. And its best if performed in front of a snookered crowd.

The whole game dinner party had been transported post cocktail hour to Hank's place up in rural New Hampshire for the main courses. He lived in an eighteenth century center chimney colonial and we would be dining in the great room, fire a' blazing. It was the perfect spot for a little end of season gluttony.

There were at least thirty of us and we'd planned a formal sit down dinner with a feast that included roasted woodcock smothered in whatever, while black duck, partridge and pheasant filled out the rest of the game side of the menu. All were prepared in interesting and exotic ways. It was the usual for sides, garlic mashed potatoes, yams, green beans, and on, and on.

We were all seated at a table assembled from several placed end to end and as the feast wrapped up and cigars were being broken out I rose for what the group presumed to be a toast to both the season and my companions in the hunt.

40

Actually, I said, "I've assembled a collection of slides I took in the field to commemorate our hunting and fishing escapades and I wanted to share these priceless moments with spouses and friends."

I directed their attention to the wall at the far end of the room. I had no slides.

I did however have one of those little clickers that I'd liberated from one of my daughters board games. You know, the brightly colored little metal clickers that produce a sharp cricket like sound when depressed and released.

So for the next fifteen minutes each time I would click the clicker and direct their attention to the next "slide" every head, without exception would turn to stare at the non-existent screen and nonexistent slide. My friends are a gullible lot.

Here's the original manuscript for the Slide Show:

Rural New Hampshire - Winter 1976

For the benefit of those of you who don't hunt, those who never experienced the thrill of bringing a wild pheasant or duck down in mid-flight which unfortunately is an experience that only rarely includes me, I've brought along some slides I took this past season to give you an idea of what it's all about when our little group goes out.

Most of the guys mistakenly thought I was carrying a 12 gage shotgun whenever we went out . . . in reality it was a 35mm camera cleverly disguised as an Ithaca pump. This of course completely explains any lack of success on my part. They would have you believe my low productivity in the field had something to do with shooting skills. . or rather my lack thereof.

Nevertheless I consider myself quite fortunate to have had the opportunity to hunt with real masters; seasoned, experienced veterans of the field . . . knowledgeable, backwoods types who could show me the ropes about bird shooting in New England. . . I just wish some of those guys could have been here tonight so you could meet them.

But let's get to the slides.

Apparently one of the first things you have to figure out when you go bird shooting in New England is in fact where to go. *(Click)* As you can see from this first slide the best spots are often off the beaten track. More often than not they are in basically uncivilized regions where only men completely committed to the hunt; men of the strongest intestinal fortitude will venture. It takes a strong stomach to go to most of these spots. To prove my point, I managed to take an interior shot of Taffy's Luncheonette *(Click)* which will give you a better idea of what I mean. Just look at those surly characters at the counter, the one on the end in particular.. .unshaven, unkempt, sneering, defiant . . . you'd never believe it to see the way Hank is dressed tonight.

Of course, any hunter worth his salt knows he has to get around and cover new territory, always explore new spots. *(Click)* This is Hazel's Last Stand & Luncheonette in West Newbury, *(Click)* Healey's, *(Click)* Kathy's Traffic Circle Restaurant in Newburyport, *(Click)* and the not soon to be forgotten Italian Sub Base in Salisbury. Incidentally, the Sub Base really earned the right to be called "Italian"...they let a sleazy dog lick plates right in front of the clientele.

Naturally, we were all outraged, (Click) particularly Willie, who you see here talking to the owner...we didn't find out until about a week later but Willie wasn't chewing the guy out...he was applying for the job. (Click) . . . here he is working the graveyard shift.

We actually did get out into the field for a little serious hunting . . . it wasn't all just eating breakfast. One of the better spots was a protected, stocked area of West Newbury where we went every Wednesday morning for pheasant. It's out by the town dump in West Newbury and is known locally as the West Newbury Olympic Pheasant Shoot and Wounded Game Preserve or the Put 'n Take for short. The only problem with the area is that it tends to be a little crowded.

(Click) here's a shot of the parking attendant

(Click) the "take a number" sign near the entrance

(Click) and Willie, proudly showing off his number "One" draw for the sixth week in a row. I'm not suggesting that Willie is overly concerned with beating the rest of us into the area every Wednesday morning, but while most hunters rely on traditional equipment like the world famous LL Bean Hunting Shoe.

(Click) here we see Willie lacing up a pair of track and field shoes.

Yup, you can learn a lot about hunting when you're lucky enough to go out with someone who's had a lot of experience. Take a basic skill like gun safety. Just learning the proper way to carry a gun is something that takes years of practice.

(Click) Here's Hank, giving the group a practical demonstration in that particular fine art as he's walking down a narrow trail. The key here is to be constantly aware of where the barrel of the gun is pointing, constantly aware of the location of your hunting companions who in this case...

(Click) are observing Hank's technique from the safety of Willie's station wagon about 50 yards away.

But back to the Put & Take (Click)

It's a beautiful piece of land, bounded on one side by private land and (Click) on the other by the West Newbury dump... oops, sorry that's the back of Jack's farm car.

The land *(Click)* is open rolling fields . . . bordered by wooded, swampy land. Stands of fallen trees and cleared brush that provides perfect cover for the elusive pheasant . . . but unfortunately when one is merely wounded these stands of brush become their graves. A "winged" pheasant will often retreat to the seclusion of the brush to die a silent, ignominious death. Bad enough that this happens. . . even with the best of hunters. . . but at least these poor helpless birds could be left in peace in the natural surroundings which were once their homes.

Now one of the group . . . who shall remain nameless ... has been known to take one of the bodies exhumed from their brushy grave and use it as a training device for his dog. Coldly tossing the lifeless creatures through the air deep into the woods (at least seven or eight feet), this callous hunter would then command his dog to "fetch up" the decomposing remains. (Pause)

Incidentally *(Click)* here's the new kennel Jack built for Louie.

Speaking of Jack . . . around the middle of the season he called to ask if I wanted to go out to Newbury and "jump" a few ducks. I'd never heard that phrase before and just assumed that it was a term used to describe a technique for hunting. Not so . . .

(Click) here's Jack hiding behind a barn in Newbury waiting for some unsuspecting duck to wander by. Discretion alone prevents me from showing the slide I took when Jack decided we should mount a couple of the ducks we jumped.

The rest of the slides are just some random snapshots taken over the course of the hunting season and require little or no explanation.

Like this one *(Click)*

Or this one *(Click)*

But seriously . . . this, my first year of bird shooting in New England, was really fun. You know everyone had told me how great it was getting outdoors, breathing the fresh air, communing with nature and I'd be the last to suggest that there was any exaggeration in what I was told. And to show my appreciation for being allowed to tag along on the hunt last season I managed to finagle membership cards for the guys in a very exclusive club. "Greater

Newburyport's Breakfast, Shooting and Sipping Society"
. . . better known as
the "BS" club.

HENRY'S PLACE
Unity, Maine – Every October from 1975 to 1985

The town of Unity, jewel of Waldo County, Maine, is best known as the home of Unity College, which the townspeople founded in 1965 in an effort to offset the economic effects of the declining chicken farming industry.

The declining people population incidentally was then, just under 2000 people; happily more than that number of woodcock seemed to pass through each October.

Speaking of chicken farmers, how 'bout them '77 Red Sox? Finishing second (again) with a record of 97 wins and 64 losses. This was once again beginning to feel a little bit like kissing your sister; close but no cigar.

The best part of the season turned out to be the fisticuffs involving Billy Martin and Reggie Jackson when the Yanks came to Fenway. Rice doubled but Martin was convinced that Jackson had given Rice the extra base by not putting in the effort to retrieve the ball quickly. The ever inflammatory Martin exploded and yanked Jackson from the game on the spot.

When Jackson made it to the dugout Martin began to read him the riot act, to which Reggie responded that Martin's propensity for alcohol made it impossible for him to exercise sound

46

judgment... or words that conveyed a message something like that.

Martin went after Reggie, outweighed and elderly by comparison. Martin's decision to do so clearly a validation of Jacksons' already clearly embraced appraisal of his manager's judgment.

Yogi and Elston Howard had to pull them apart. To which Yogi is rumored to have muttered. "It ain't over 'til it's over... and this one's over!"

To their everlasting delight Sox fans all over the nation saw this play out thanks to a camera man who never flinched.

The Sox won 4 to 1.

Henry's place was a stark, somewhat unkempt, partially but for the most part un-restored farmhouse in rural Unity, Maine.

I realize that saying "rural Unity, Maine" is redundant. In downtown Unity a traffic jam consisted of being stuck behind one car at the only traffic light in town. On the plus side, we also quickly learned should your turn signal fail it really wouldn't matter since everyone in town seemed to know where we were going anyway.

Henry's house was a mid to late 19th century homestead having the obligatory attached barn, a dog friendly front porch adorned with rocker and an unkempt field to the rear. The place burned to the ground in the mid 80's, several years past our last visit, and sadly a double wide subsequently took its place.

Henry's had an antique Glenwood cooking and heating stove which was the dominant feature in an altogether very pleasant country kitchen, replete with a walk- in pantry, window overlooking the veggie garden and the indoor companion to the outdoor rocking chair.

It had a tin roof to help lull the partially inebriated among us to sleep on gently rainy evenings, as if we needed any lulling. Best of all it was in close proximity to some spectacular bird covers all included in the package price of free.

In addition to serving the more mundane functions of heating and cooking, the wood stove was also pretty handy at drying out wet bird dogs at the end of a hunt. We would simply stack them like flapjacks neatly in front of the stove taking occasional care to make sure that none burst spontaneously into flame.

Nothing beats the scent of musty, drying dog hair fresh from a roll in a cow flop.

Life is good.

The trip itself up to Henry's place had become a ritual that included equal parts Bourbon and black coffee sometimes complimented by a heady, wafting aroma that would emerge from the backseat. It was the result of gastrointestinal distress emanating from a 120 lb black lab whose nerves and digestive track had been churning overtime in anticipation of the upcoming week of hunting.

Whew!

These trips to Unity were usually made under cover of darkness escaping suburban Boston in a rusty GMC Suburban hunt mobile which cut a 75 mph swath through the Maine turnpike blackness toward Augusta. After about two hours we'd bang a right and head on up to Unity and the land of feathery expectations.

On the dark side, staying at Henry's place meant being civil to a couple of locals that Henry had befriended. So in reality I guess there really was a price we paid. One in particular was Arnold, a linesman for Maine Power who proved paradoxically to be a both a nice guy and a pathological liar. When it came to sharing information about decent hunting covers in the area, he simply couldn't bring himself to point us in the right direction.

Our theory was that he was fearful of directing us to his "good" covers thinking that would result in our cleaning them out. This erroneous assumption could have been put immediately to rest if he had simply accompanied us on one trip afield. He would have been immediately reassured that since none of us were crack shots the local bird population would remain safe and more likely would be merely amused not threatened by our presence.

What we never quite figured out was that Arnold would almost always arrive to greet us within 30 minutes or so of our arrival, which I would remind you, was almost always in the pitch black of night.

Among our theories was one that had the toll attendant at the last booth on the Maine pike either a paid informant or first cousin of Arnold's who gave him a quick call and a heads up as we pulled through the toll gate and off the turnpike for the final run to Henry's place. No paranoid personalities here.

He was actually a pretty decent guy. One year he even invited us over for a big lasagna spread with "the family".

It's just that he somehow got perverse pleasure in making sure we endlessly chased our tails around in the most unproductive covers he knew. And since our group had always been filled with slow learners, Arnold knew he was working very fertile ground. We pretty much went wherever he told us to go; the Dixmont dump, the Unity dump, d'dump, d'dump, d'dump, d'dump.

Brighter men would have fallen for this misdirection once and only once, or as President Dub-Ya was so fond of saying "Fool me once, shame on you, fool me twice and … then… uh, you can fool me a whole bunch more times or something like that."

Anyway, fools that we were, one of the more memorable little jaunts Arnold sent us on was a screech of dawn duck hunt down to the Carlton Bog. The lesson I ultimately took away from this experience was never to hunt in a place called a bog to begin with. It took me a little longer to conclude that I should also never hunt in a place that ends with the word "dump" as well.

Carlton Bog was in actuality less bog than pond. Admittedly, the approach to where we would set up our "blind" was a little swampy but no match for a 16 foot shiny aluminum canoe.

In a fashion similar to our historic crossing of the Merrimack River which you'll learn of later, Willie, Jack and I along with the Grabber, the big lab, headed down to the bogs edge before sun up to see if we could bag a couple of mallards.

It was however what we used to call a "blue bird day", so named for the crystal clear skies that would have encouraged a variety of tweety birds to cruise comfortably in the rising sunlight as it bounced in blinding reflection off the sides of our aluminum craft, but on ducks.

Fortunately, we arrived at a little island in the middle of the bog just before what we hoped would be scores of incoming ducks. Trouble was they weren't incoming to us. Seems we had picked, or rather Arnold had directed us to the one spot in the bog that was anathema to waterfowl, judging by their avoidance of same.

Still the coffee was hot(ish) even though the day was chilly... as in very chilly. It was in this quiet, reflective, early morning moment that yet another brilliant scheme popped into my somewhat addled head. Battery-operated heated socks.

This was only one of a number of brilliant ideas that would ensue that evening as we entertained ourselves by conceiving of the Duckmoor Catalog of Outdoor Sporting Paraphernalia.

Our plan was to go head to toe against the more famous L.L. people by offering products that no one else had. Battery-operated heated socks we resolved quickly should be immediately adopted as the new company's loss leader. Then we were stuck.

Eventually, the best second idea we could come up with was to offer Mr. Duckmoor's famous pre-ripped waders on the theory that saving anglers the irritation of having to do to themselves what was inevitable would be an attractive selling proposition.

Perhaps brilliant is too strong a word.

We lasted on the island waiting for ducks for about an hour before resignation set in and finally piled back into the canoe for the return trip.

Now here's the part that struck me funny. No sooner did we start paddling back the hundred and fifty yards or so to the car than ducks began to appear in both large and small numbers, flying overhead like gnats.

They were still out of range but being the perpetual optimists and fools that we were, we somehow thought they would ignore the bright glare of our canoe, the yelping of the Grabber and despite both distractions decide to settle in near us. Thus, as each duck flew over during the next few minutes we would scrunch down effectively reducing our profile by about 2 inches, as if this would help. Help it did not.

But the reaction to each bird that flew over was the same.

Three guys in a bright silver canoe, hoping the ducks were of the brainless variety.

SPEAKING OF LIFE IN MAINE...

Among the many outdoor sporting activities Maine has to offer aside from quality fishing and hunting is that of amusing its visitors with observations of the Maine life, its' people, its' landscape, its' peccadilloes.

It began for us when we discovered that the Maine Exterior Lawn Decorators Society's annual showcase and pro-am competition seemed to coincide each fall with our arrival for a little birding. The competitors seemed to always pull out all the stops in pursuit of the state's top lawn decorating honors.

The rules were simple enough, cover every inch of your lawn, and I use the term "lawn" loosely, with objects that once had functional value but had succumbed at last to the rust bug and needed to be put out to pasture. Consequently, some of the most memorable entries were not just the rather mundane and predictable rusty 1964 Chevy truck carefully striking a haughty pose, wheels removed, perched on blocks, surrounded by tread-bare piles of tires, but those where those same vintage cars were gaily set off by overturned refrigerators, one-hinged dryers and the occasional toaster oven tossed in to add that special touch.

Each year we took it upon ourselves to make special mention of particularly engaging displays as we plied the back roads in search of birds.

An honorable mention one year went to Lloyd Bickford, the man who, you may recall had for so long ungraciously deprived Howard of his rightful spot in the Maine Cap Hall of Fame.

Lloyd's winning entry was a nice arrangement which included a defunct antique washer with top wringer unpretentiously leaning against the disembodied rusty bed of a pickup both blocking the front door of his house.

Just a thought: auto repair and breakfast eateries seem to be the underpinnings of the Maine economy. And why is it that every able or unable bodied man in Maine eats breakfast wearing a camouflage hat? And if the camo hats really worked, how is possible that I would know they're wearing them? Or how in fact would I even know that they were there eating breakfast? Too many questions; not enough answers!

UNCOMMON HILL
Thorndike, Maine – October 1977

It had only been two years since the disappointment of the seven game match-up with the Cincinnati Reds and still a year away from the unmentionable BFD episode.

Between the two the 1977 Red Sox get lost in the sauce. It was one of the all time great teams, and with the exception of a weak bat at second base the Sox put an amazingly tough line up on the field.

Rice was already a veteran, at least he was putting up veteran numbers and playing like one averaging .320 with 39 homers

Having Yaz, Pudge, Hobson and Lynn in the dressing room at the same time sure beat a poke in the eye with a sharp stick.. In the end the Sox were, however, once again relegated to a second place finish by the Bronx guys.

By mid-October the Fenway crowd was a speck in the rear view mirror.

We made a promise at the Puddin' Mill that year... "No matter where we might find ourselves we would all meet up again in front of the old cabin when we turned fifty".

It seemed so far away at the time.

Common Hill is a vast bird cover assessable down an abandoned road where at one time stately maples and oaks framed the entries to colonial farmhouses.

Each had tasty little orchards in their backyards to serve the needs of the farm families that lived there. Many of those orchards still survive, still bearing fruit, more importantly attracting grouse.

Perhaps ten or more such farms were located along the three or four miles of the now severely washed out road that runs through Common Hill. The maples, oaks and orchards are still there but now only mark the spots that once were the entrances to farmhouses. All that's left of long ago deserted farmhouses are their foundations now fallen in on themselves.

There was nothing common about Common Hill if you like upland hunting. It was another shooter's paradise which proved very difficult to for us to discover considering the lack of help we were getting from the locals.

Arnold in particular had gone out of his way to divert our attention from this area. And even when we were about to stumble on it accidentally he just happened to be there to try to lead us astray one last time.

We made a habit of doing a little exploration on each trip to try and locate new covers. Areas change, growth matures and unless cut back periodically eventually becomes less attractive to birds.

Occasionally "No Hunting" signs pop up on a previously accessible cover, or a hunters' shack is erected forcing us to move on.

It was on one of those exploratory missions that we pulled up behind a familiar pick up, Arnold's. At first he was nowhere to be seen, then rustling through the brush about twenty yards down what was clearly a well worn path across a little stream Arnold emerged, shotgun in hand.

We all later agreed that having a camera to record the look on his face as he realized that we'd caught him coming out of one of his special covers would have been priceless.

It took him only a moment to recover.

"Boys!", he stammered.

Everyone in Maine called us "boys". "Sorry I got in here ahead of you. I bumped a couple of woodcock but the cover is so small you'll not likely see much more."

"What's down the path?" Willie inquired.

"Not much. Runs out in about a hundred yards, the first twenty-five or so on the right is about all I ever hunt. This is one of a couple little spots I poke my head in and out of on the way home from work. Didn't mention it since I didn't think it would be worth your time."

We glanced at one another, the first rays becoming visible from the light bulbs finally going on in our heads as each of us fought back the urge to shout "Liar, liar pants on fire!!!"

"Well" we said, "long as we're here we might as well give the dogs a run."

He seemed unsettled with the prospect that we were going to hunt this "small" area despite his lackluster endorsement..

"Suit your selves" he said. "Gotta get home." And with that Arnold and Arnold's pick up drove into the late October afternoon setting sun.

We had about a half hour of hunting left before sunset and decided to push down the path a little. As it turned out the path did not end in about 100 yards but opened into an area known locally as the "Puddin' Mill". Cock-o-block full of partridge, the Puddin' Mill would have to wait 'til next year since we had discovered the area at the end of our hunt on Saturday, the day before our departure.

It still took us two more years to figure out that continuing down a path or road could produce spectacular results. The Puddin' Mill was at the foothills of Common Hill, both subsequently providing years of shooting entertainment.

Common Hill was also the location of the second major flight of woodcock I would experience. We had grown more sophisticated in the trinkets we carried through the woods. I had a flush counter with two numbered rotating drums that would let me keep track of the number of birds we pushed on any given outing. Turn one drum to count woodcock, one to count partridge.

Large sections of the Hill had been clear cut about five years or so before we discovered it and were only now being repopulated mostly by maples. The saplings were thick as thieves and presented a real challenge as we worked the autumn hillside.

In 1982, the year in question, we had dubbed the saplings maple whips since they stood about eyeball high and had the annoying tendency to spring back into their natural position as we pushed through, slapping our shins, butts and knees and noses.

'82 had been an all around good year for woodcock hunting with their numbers up and we were looking forward to a full days hunt on Common Hill. This meant bringing a cooler stuffed with liverwurst sammies smothered with red onion on rye, a few brew and a selection from Mr. Doritio's private reserve.

Almost immediately we were into a flight. In the space of about an hour and half my trusty counter had logged 71 flushes. No doubt there were actually fewer than that number of birds there since we were clearly pushing some of them back and forth.

Still another flight. My second, thereby full filling what must surely prove to be my quota for life.

DON'T GIVE ME ANY BULL!
...bovines, moose or otherwise
West Kennebec, Maine – October 1978

September is normally a time of great expectations for an upland hunter. At the All Star break we expected our Sox to walk away with it.

In '78 we were subjected to what has become know as the Boston Massacre. The Sox managed to blow a fourteen game lead at the break and came back to Fenway just four up on the Yankees. We all prayed for a sweep of the Bombers that would have put them away for good but secretly we would have been happy to split and just preserve that four game lead.

It was another pleasant afternoon at Howard's as we were wrapping up another pleasant upland adventure.

We came to a fence on the other side of which stood a rather formidable looking bull. I say a rather formidable looking bull as if any bull I've ever seen was something less than formidable looking. They pretty much all fall into that category.

This gave us (the uninitiated in basic animal husbandry) pause to contemplate whether the smarter, more prudent path to the other side of the field might not just be to follow the barbed wire fence line taking care to keep it between us and the bull. The fence was barely visible next to the wood line which was overgrown with secondary brush mostly of the prickly variety. Even given the obvious inconvenience this seemed like the best course of action.

While we stood there still carefully formulating the particulars of our avoidance strategy Jack slipped gingerly over the fence and proceeded without so much as a "how do you do" or a glance at the bull as he lumbered across the field.

Willie, a salesman by both nature and profession couldn't help but observe, "Sure he's not afraid of that bull but I'd like to see how fearless he would be taking some of my customers out for a martini lunch."

Another Axiom of the hunt: Find very funny people to share these times with. There's nothing that can take the curse off the occasionally empty game pouch or fishing creel like a good laugh.

PUTTING A DENT IN OPENING DAY
Greenland, New Hampshire – Monday, October 2, 1978

To paraphrase Chuck Dickens "It was the best of days it was the worst of days". It was in fact opening day for woodcock which ordinarily fell on the first of October.

The only variation is when the first falls on a Sunday. So TC and I piled into his Suburban and headed up to Howard's that Monday.

In July the Yankees found themselves behind the Red Sox the aforementioned 14 games in the AL East.

Steinbrenner, itching to make a change fired Billy Martin and offered the managerial slot to Bob Lemon.

By September the Yankees came to Fenway for a four game series, and the Sox fourteen game lead had been reduced to a measly four games. The incredible shrinking lead was about to become the incredible disappearing lead.

The Yankees took the first game 15-3 led by a five RBI game from Willie Randolph and the second by pounding the Sox 13-2. Ron Guidry added insult to injury tossing a shut out in game three and then mopped up on Sunday 7-4. In seven weeks they came all the way back to tie the Sox for first.

So, competing for our attention by October was the now extinct one game play off between New York and Boston for the best record in the American League East. Both ended the season with identical 99–63 records. That four game lead had become history. A flip of a coin gave the Sox an undeserved home team advantage.

Guidry started for NY while Mike Torrez took the hill for Boston. Yaz gave them a two run lead with a home run followed by a RBI on a Rice single. In the top of the seventh, with two on Yankee shortstop Bucky Dent popped a Torrez pitch just over the Green Monster.

Munson brought another run home with a double in the 7th and Reggie homered in the 8th. It was 5-2 Yanks

The Sox struggled back 5-4 in the 8th on singles by Yaz and Lynn, but the "Goose" Gossage shut them down.

The hunting that day exceeded our expectations; hard to do since our expectations were always sky high. Neither Reuben, my well intended but only marginally talented English setter, and Louie, Jack's German wire-haired pointer had ever given either of us any reasons to write home.

On the other hand, neither dog had run away. Both were now safely tucked into their kennels for the ride home. Topping off this typically very pleasant first day of the '78 season we headed back with full larders of woodcock, the game already past inning five on the radio.

There are certain events in life, the assassinations of JFK, Robert and Martin Luther King, man's first landing on the moon where you can recount in extraordinary detail where you were and what the weather was like down to the last Fahrenheit when you heard the news.

We were westbound on the Portsmouth Road approaching the swing around where it joins route 108 coming out of Newmarket. I had one boot propped over the glove compartment on Jack's dash. It was 71 degrees.

The Black Monday Playoff dashed any hopes or dreams with a homer in the top of the seventh inning by Bucky F. Dent. It was one of only five home runs he would hit that season.

Even woodcock pie and a little loud mouth soup was unable to provide sufficient comfort

PS
The Yankees won the first two, blowing out the Sox 15-3 and 13-2.

The Nation then sucked it up with the confidence that leading with you best shot, the Eck, brings. Then in game three watched Dennis get pounded.

THE PUT & TAKE
West Newbury, Massachusetts - Thursday, November 2, 1978

The Boston Massacre was behind us but the memory lingers on!

Pheasant hunting at the Crane's Pond stocking area, variously the West Newbury Olympic Pheasant Shoot and Wounded Game Preserve or as it was more commonly known the "Put and Take" was a little bit like an Easter egg hunt for grown ups. The fish and game folks would hide pheasant every Tuesday evening at dusk and we would go out with our dogs and find them the following morning. I half expected, upon cleaning the birds after the hunt to discover they had creamy chocolate fillings.

It was the hunter's equivalent of chicken take-out, lacking only a drive through window. The playing field would have been, as they say leveled if it had simply been an old fashioned duel.

This embarrassingly easy pheasant harvest reached an absurd level one November morning when the Grabber, a 120 pound black Labrador Retriever who was particularly adroit at finding, flushing then leaping at rapidly and snatching them in mid air brought three back to the car before Willie, his chauffer, had even taken his gun out of its case.

Willie never even went in to the area that day or for that matter ever again. He just zipped his gun back into its case, kenneled the Grabber and went home for eggs, toast and sausage.

It turned out, however, that the Put & Take would prove to be more versatile than just being an overnight repository for pheasant.

When I first moved to West Newbury, our then next door neighbors were a couple who in an effort to fully embrace the country lifestyle had acquired a farmyard menagerie consisting of a number of laying hens, a rooster, two sheep, a goat and a turkey who clearly was going through some sort of identify crisis from hanging exclusively with chickens.

As tenants not owners of the property, once they needed to move it quickly became apparent that finding another landlord willing to accommodate their barnyard of pets that included both their feathered and other friends was not going to happen.

In a gesture that they no doubt thought of as generosity I came home from work the day they moved and found a wire cage stuffed with the aforesaid chickens and one cranky old rooster along with a note attached that simply read "Enjoy". Apparently they decided to take the turkey along.

After two days a steady drum of clucking and pecking became the final straw. I woke up just once too often to the melodic sounds of the rooster crowing and to the realization that I could not keep these birds. I tried to give them away.

Even Crazy Harold, the dog catcher in the next town over thumbed his nose at the offer and he was a fellow who would normally jump at any chance to fill his family's larder with free grub. It seems that even the finest laying hens eventually get so long in the tooth that a chicken stock fate might be their last best shot at culinary immortality.

My solution? I took them to Crane's Pond just after the stocking agents had dropped off their usual bakers dozen of pheasant one Tuesday evening and liberated the chicken, thereby permitting them to join forces with their more colorful cousins. As the sun was setting, I watched the little gaggle of hens tentatively stroll into their brave new world, led of course by a strutting, soon to be crow-less rooster.

I couldn't resist and got there early the next morning in time to see a couple of dandies from Revere. They were driving a pitch black Camaro with flames adorning each side, also complimented by a pair of sponge dice bobbing below the rear view.

Two young men in hunter's orange jump suits emerged for the mornings hunt. They had brought along a young Revere lass also attired in orange but sans gun. I suppose she was there to retrieve downed birds since they had no dog.

Unfortunately, cell phone cameras were still nearly three decades away. I didn't stick around to see if any of the recently liberated chicken would be topping the menu at a dinner table somewhere in Revere preferring instead to let that amusing fantasy linger as it has for lo these many years.

RETREIVING THE RETREVER
West Kennebec, Maine – Wednesday, October 11, 1979

A man, his dog, a little sciatica and a struggling New York Yankee lineup make for a perfect day out in the field.

I had the dog, a little sciatica and in '79 the Yankees finished in fourth place, 13.5 games behind the Orioles. It was the end of their three year assault on the American League East.

This despite off-season moves that included acquiring veteran hurlers Tommy John and Luis (yes, our Louie) Tiant both available through free agency,

Nothing much went right for the Bombers. Goose missed a big chunk of the season after injuring his hand in a clubhouse scuffle with Cliff Johnson. Catfish Hunter, Figueroa, and Gullen also were injured along with Nettles, Mickey Rivers and to the enormous delight of The Nation… Bucky Dent.

Our Sox? Third place; surely this must be a strategic move no doubt intended to position them for "next year" by lulling the Yanks into overconfidence.

I once had a golden retriever named Jason. The guy was both a sweetheart, and for one fleeting moment in time, a primo hunting dog. He was a dog of gentile temperament, possessing all the requisite tennis ball instincts associated with his breed. For the most part he never displayed any interest in birds but would rather have us throw sticks or balls on our strolls through the woods.

Not long after hooking up with my bird shooting companions, I got serious about acquiring a bird dog as my first love had become woodcock and partridge hunting where a pointing dog, at least in theory could be a real asset. I say "could" since even experienced gun dogs have trouble holding a skittish partridge for more than a moment or two.

And so, the first in what would become a series of unruly English setters, Rube, joined our family and began to join me in the alders. Having never trained a bird dog before, my lack of skill in that area stuck out every time we went out like the proverbial sore thumb.

Not really the dogs fault, but like most hunters I laid the blame for many a missed opportunity on his too range-y behavior squarely at his paws anyway.

This lasted for most of the first two seasons we hunted together until one day… Why not Jason?

Why not indeed? All the while it had never occurred to me that my galumpho housedog Jason might turn out to have some hunting instincts. No, I couldn't expect him to point but we'd been hunting over a black lab for years who always managed to give us ample warning before busting a bird.

So the next Saturday, on a perfectly brisk and sunny late October morning, I left Rube at home and with Jason and the Grabber tucked into the back of Willies' wagon trekked on up to Howard's for an afternoon hunt.

Jason would be hunting that day side-by-side with The Grabber, a 120 pound black lab and a veteran of the Kennebunk cover we were headed to. The Grabber immediately took Jason under his wing leading him to the closest cow flop in the field for the traditional manure roll that was a ritual part of each hunt. He seemed eager for the hunt so having fitted him with a sparkling new orange collar and bell we headed into the "hot" corner to see if we could find a couple of timber doodles.

Within no more than a minute or two he began acting strangely, literally shaking over what turned out to be the intoxicating smell (to him) of the little critter hiding beneath the first batch of alders we approached.

"Willie", I said. "This could be good. He's acting birdy"

No sooner said then BOOM!!! The woodcock exploded from his hiding place and headed for parts unknown.

I missed with both barrels but Willie covered my mistakes.

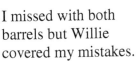

Imagine that! Right under my nose all those years a well-behaved hunting dog that actually came when I called, had a great nose for birds and didn't range too far. It's true he wasn't the classic upland pointer capable of holding a statuesque pose for minutes as a time but this was surely the next best thing. Upon finding a bird he had no apparent interest in flushing them out, content to announce their presence with a near convulsive shaking motion that provided more than adequate notice that a bird was at hand.

We spent the next half hour with the same scene playing itself out four or five more times. This dog was terrific!

He did however seem to have a peculiar way of looking at me over his shoulder each time I shot at a bird. In retrospect kind of like "What the...was that!"

Then, on bird six or seven, suddenly he was gone. Without so much as a howdy-do Jason disappeared while Willie and I were busy looking for the bird we just brought down. For the next hour we searched not for the bird but for Jason. We called, called again, searched then continued to do that a whole lot more. I was not looking forward to returning home sans our beloved pet.

Slowly we worked our way back toward the car thinking we'd take a break then resume looking in the afternoon where we discovered Jason sitting patiently by the tailgate waiting for his ride home. Puzzled but relieved we headed right back into the covers.

It didn't take long until he was doing his shake-y thing having located another woodcock. But this time when I came up behind him to flush the bird he turned and in a slow gait began to trot across the open field. I called for him to come. All I got was a glance over his shoulder without so much as a hitch in his gait.

No amount of calling, pleading or cajoling brought him around. He trotted and glanced back each time I called his name, then when he saw me begin to run after him he broke into a nervous gallop followed by a panic stricken dead run clearly trying to put as much distance as he could between us.

His mission apparently did not include more time in the field.

In stunned realization, Willie and I turned to each other and in unison chimed "Gun shy!" a very distressing epithet to end a short lived canine hunting career.

The only good part of this outing was that Willie was too busy laughing to snap a picture of me chasing Jason across the field resulting in a classic Pursuit and Tackle.

BEWARE PACTS OF DOGS

I am convinced that there is a pact among dogs, a vow of silence whereby they enter into a life-long covenant not to reveal that they not only understand every word we say but are also capable of clearly speaking the King's English.

To understand the reason that this is not widely know you need merely to consider the consequences were this well kept secret to get out…they might actually have to behave!
You would only have to explain things once, like "Here's the deal, Esmeralda. We go to the cover together then you stay within sight of me. Smell a bird, point it. I shoot it… you go bring it back. There'll be food in a shiny metal dish on the floor back at the cabin if all goes according to plan.

That way everybody's happy, no apoplectic fits and displays of sobbing by a grown man.

Deal?"

IRISH SETTERS ARE TO HUNTING AS TEETH ARE TO HENS *(superfluous)*

Hank's newest hunting dog, Jet the Irish Setter, resolved once and for all the issue as to whether his breed had retained any of its ancestral hunting instinct or had been seduced to the rangy ways and influence of their obvious soul mates the Greyhound. I'm not saying he was a far-ranging dog but one time on a hunt in northern Maine he disappeared long enough that upon his return he commenced barking in French and we had to peel a bunch of Canadian border inspection stickers off his back.

We've also had our share of "runners", dogs who performed a disappearing act the moment we would arrive at a cover. Jack's English Pointer, Belle was a runner. She'd be off the moment the tailgate dropped, her little bell quickly becoming a distant memory. Now and again she'd make what came to be known as a cameo appearance as she ran by determined not to acknowledge us, still hard at work looking for birds, nose to the grindstone.

Over time we finally realized that Belle had one of the finest noses in New England and was merely irritated that she was forced to accompany a bunch of rookie hunters every time she went out who clearly were only slowing her down.

We concluded therefore that the ideal pointing dog would clearly be one with Belle's hunting instincts and nose but one whose legs had been temporarily anesthetized just prior to the hunt permitting us to then outfit them with a carrying strap, much like a piece of luggage which you could carry through the woods or suspend beneath your gun.

No running… the dog could then merely be used like a Geiger counter, sniffing, stiffening, twitching and eventually pointing as we carried her through the woods until we came upon a bird.

THE GREATER KENNEBUNK OPEN
West Kennebunk, Maine – Saturday, October 13, 1979

Along Alfred Road in West Kennebunk there used to be a "one-stop", probably still there. Petrol for the hunt mobile, Hostess Cup Cakes, pocket knives, a floor-to-ceiling cooler full of beer and soda, hunters' orange caps – no surprise since I've yet to find a gas station in either New Hampshire or Maine that doesn't sell them.

Best of all they specialized in making up game pocket sized sub sandwiches. It became therefore a mandatory stop on the way to Howard's.

The final somewhat depressing order of finish that year had Baltimore in first, followed by Milwaukee, Boston in third and, oh yeah, the Yankees.

It's true, misery does love company.

Saturday, October 12, 1979, a moment of epic upland hunting history although technically a part of the Howard saga deserved special mention. It was the day the migratory woodcock flight to end all flights became known as the "Greater Kennebunk Open".

"Flights" of woodcock, the unexpected arrival in large numbers in one location of woodcock has been surrounded by myth and lore for the hunting crew for years.

The idea to an upland shootist that large numbers of birds might all arrive in one area at the same time and be there when they arrive, guns and dogs in hand triggers the proverbial chill along the spine action.

We were on our way to Henry's Place in Unity, Maine for our annual week of bird shooting and bourbon sipping and had left early in order to allow time for the mandatory stop and a morning shoot at Howard's on the way up.

The fall color at the farm looked as if Lassell Ripley, his very own self, had just completed a quick touch up for our benefit. Decorated in crimson, orange, sporting a full palette of traditional fall colors the woods were particularly inviting that early October morning. The air was, as they say, crisp and so were the leaves under our feet. Both the dogs and the hunters were jumpy, anxious to see what little feathered surprises the alder thickets and aspen stands might hold.

Little did we know we were about to take a short cut to woodcock nirvana. Our route into our standard covers at Howard's took us about fifty yards along a barbed fence line that separated a ragged pasture from some second growth hardwoods. Our group consisted of five guys with marginal shooting ability plus three dogs. We gave the lead position and first shot to our special guest from the tidewaters of Maryland, Frank the surgeon who could distinguish between a black duck and a mallard in fight but it turned out seemed to have only limited exposure to the wily ways and erratic flight of the woodcock.

Since every memorable trip needs a little mirth as a send-off it was appropriate that we hadn't walked ten yards before Belle, the only one of the dogs who had uncharacteristically chosen to stay in range, put on the brakes and drew up into her best, fancy English Pointer point. Her nose, as previously mentioned was as good as they get. In fact so good we used to say she could point at a spot where a bird was going to land but hadn't quite gotten to yet.

Ok, Frank. First one's yours". We generously offered.

With that and in front of an appreciative audience of four Frank proceeded to walk up the bird, subsequently trying the less direct approach to hunting of having the noise of the shot scare the bird to death. That failing he then followed the first shot with the traditional, ceremonial second shot as the bird flitted away to warn its' buddies of our arrival.

For the next twenty minutes or so we wandered in and out of fields and alder bunches pushing the occasional bird, bagging a couple, missing more and admiring the spectacular day we were having the good fortune to play around in.

It was about 11am when we reached the power lines, a slash and burn swathe cut through the farm by Maine Power to accommodate its lines.

Minimally maintained, the easement passed through a low, somewhat soggy corner right at the northwest edge of the farm. The semi-permanent wet conditions had encouraged the growth of about a seventy-five foot long stand of alders, neatly grouped in clumps that allowed both hunters and dogs the room to negotiate through them with ease.

This stand was big enough for five hunters to sweep through without fear of getting on the receiving end of each other's bird shot. The plan called for us to line up at the west end of the alder run, then with the precision of safari beaters, we were to proceed with reckless abandon into the fray.

Almost immediately the dogs bumped a couple of birds which elicited a couple of shots.
Two birds down.

Then, oddly the dogs didn't move to retrieve the game as they normally would. They just ran a couple more steps and pointed again. Several more birds took off and a couple more shots were fired.
More birds down.

This went on for about fifteen minutes with more birds flying and a few more falling. Even my somewhat dyslectic English Setter Ruben got in on the pointing. What I was convinced he actually had was *audible* dyslexia as evidenced by the fact that he clearly hears the command "come" to sound something like "run for the hills".

He is known in our circles affectionately as the "flying Rubenie", but that's a story for another day. In all no one got a limit, but everyone got a few birds.

Once the dust settled we guessed that at least twenty to twenty-five birds had been huddled together in the cover when we arrived.

Sometimes you eat the bear and sometimes the bear eats you.

This turned out to be a pretty good bear eating day.

THE THIRD ANNUAL
WEST KENNEBUNK OPEN
October 1st through November 30, 1978

Preregistered gunners
Sign-in begins at 9 am at the
HOWARD C. BURNSIDE MEMORIAL
RUSTY SUBURBAN RECEPTION HALL
WOODCOCK FLIGHTS SCHEDULED
TO ARRIVE DAILY AT DUSK

ON OTHER MATTERS RELATIVE TO
UPLAND HUNTING DOGS

Bird dogs are a lot smarter than some hunters are inclined to admit. In fact there's a lot we could learn from them if we'd just pay attention.

For instance, their seeming inability to hear or respond to our constant pleas to stay within sight or at least within ear-shot when in the field is probably purposeful.

Savvy hunters would be well advised to judiciously apply this behavior to the communication issues many of us encounter at home when life invariably forces a confrontation between the "honey do" list and the "honey can I do" football game.

Another thing about bird dogs is the number of rituals they go through as they warm up for the hunt.

There's the traditional "sniff out and roll in the manure" start to every hunt which I mentioned. This is almost always followed by the "lets sniff every butt in the crowd" maneuver. The trouble with the latter is that since they are in fact still dogs they will still want to lick your face.

Another revelation concerning the real utility of hunting dogs dawned on us only after years of intense research, trial and error. We came to understand what the quintessential piece of Maine grouse hunting equipment should be, a black lab that could drive a pick up truck leaving its' owner free to grease a bird or two through the window from the comfort of the "shotgun" position.

As aging uplanders, we had discovered the value of working the roads for birds, occasionally on foot, more and more frequently by vehicle. It would have been the cat's or more accurately the dog's pajamas to have someone, a trusted hunting companion steering the truck down those lonesome back roads freeing us up to potshot a grouse or two out for their evening constitutional. Wardens take note: we would never (wink, wink) grease a pa'trige from the comfort of a pickups bench seat but we suspect this is a favorite sport of many locals.

Of course, we speculated that with our luck any dog we tried to train to operate a pickup would no doubt end up not gun shy, but Ford F150 shy... back to square one.

SHOULDA SEEN THE ONE THAT DIDN'T EVEN TRY TO GET AWAY
Dartmouth Outing Club, Errol, New Hampshire – May 1980

Don Zimmer, aka Elmer Fudd led the mighty Sox to a depressing fifth place finish this year. Worse was the fact that they were 19 games behind the Yankees.

Lynn, Remy and Butch Hobson were out for long stretches along with Yaz and Rice also putting in a little time on the DL. But the main event of the '80 season was actually a post-season event.

The Sox failed to extend contracts to Pudge Fisk and Fred Lynn by the deadline.

Eventually Lynn went to the California Angels in a trade, while Fisk changed his Sox from red to white and headed out to Chicago.

Zimmer was rumored to have remarked, "Shhh! be ver-we, ver-we quiet, I'm hunting wabbits. Huuuuh"

The Dartmouth Outing Club is just a hop, skip, jump and a quick left along Route 16 just north of Errol, New Hampshire. On our first and only trip to the DOC we stayed at the Peaks Cabin a 1950's era rustic sitting on the confluence of the Dead and Swift Diamond Rivers.

The cabin could accommodate up to twelve sleepy fishermen or for that matter twelve wide awake fishermen. It came replete with gas lights, one woodstove for heating and one for cooking... one very fine, very salty place. But any description of the Peaks wouldn't be complete without mention of its best amenity; a twenty foot long front porch with rockers just spitting distance from the edge of the river.

Not twenty yards downstream from the cabin was a falls with sufficient drop to carry any full grown man into some wicked, watery places... bumps, bruises and contusions guaranteed.

As spectacular a spot as the D.O.C. was it produced very little in the way of results for nearly two days. The fish were exclusively of the brook trout persuasion and shared a annoying propensity for stunted growth that quickly bordered on the tedious.

On the last morning we broke out our gear, slipped into waders and boots and with somewhat diminished optimism once again donned our lucky fishing hats. From streamside right in front of the cabin we could see a number of smallish brookies darting in and out from under the shade of a clump of overhanging alders on the far bank.

Willie was already in up to his knees, a #14 Royal Wulff cinched to the end of his leader. The fly dangled carelessly into the still water next to his knees amidst a tangled pile of leader and line in the still backwater where we stood. He was distracted from the task at hand... fishing... by the more important ritual of firing up his pipe. Priorities are after all the first order of business among the fly fishing set.

Then Willie noticed his birds' nest of a leader mysteriously beginning to make its way upstream. Turned out a nice 12 inch brookie had taken the Wulff hook, line and well... you know the rest.

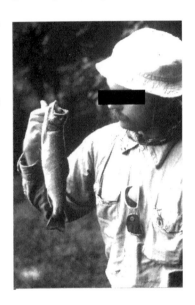

This clearly required no skill whatever on the part of Willie who commented that he's glad he decided to go with the Royal Wulff since his first impulse was to tie on a cigarette butt he'd noticed on the stream bank.

It seems there are times in life when technique simply gives way to dumb luck.

"DEAD EYE" AT THE GRAVEL PIT
Thorndike, Maine – Saturday, October 22, 1980

Some classic players hit the diamond in 1980; but before the dust settled at seasons end on contract issues the eventually to be gone Fisk and his also departing pal Fred Lynn joined Burleson, Remy and Hopson in creating another classic Boston finish; fifth place with 83 wins for the season

We've each tried the "surround 'em" technique when your dog is birdy and working a cover and it's clear that some smarty pants woodcock or grouse is about to make a clever dash for parts unknown. A dash I should point out that is frequently successful. The "surround 'em" technique for the record is merely "you take that side" of the cover "and I'll take this".

I know for those of you who don't hunt this may seem a little like the ill advised concept of a circular firing squad but that logic has never dissuaded bird shooters from employing the technique.

In addition to having tried this technique, every hunter has also experienced the embarrassment of taking a clear surround 'em shot and combining it consequently with a clean miss in full view of eyewitnesses.

Enter stage left Ernie who by accident of the spot he happened to be standing in along the road when the dogs got birdy was about to be blessed with several shooting opportunities, and cursed with several witnesses.

Not often, but occasionally partridge are nudged by a dog, one at a time from their cover, only to fly away lazily as if being air born was the only protection they needed, not a speedy retreat.

Such was the case of birds in a small thicket next to a gravel pit and the old cemetery on the way to the Puddin' Mill.

These birds were about to pop out, one by one onto the road, each hanging a right and proceeding to glide down into the wide open area of the gravel pit. It would be like shooting fish in a barrel. It should be noted that sometimes shooting fish in a barrel can be very tricky.

The Grabber, the most senior member of our cadre of hunting dogs, holding the honorary position of hunting dog crew chief was doing due diligence snooping for birds as we quietly approached the gravel pit. On the other side of the pit were the remnants of a fallen in foundation and small orchard that we and several partridge of the feathered persuasion frequented.

As if on cue, the dog got birdy and began to root around at the base of a thicket. By reason of where he happened to be standing, Ernie's deli number came up. This would be his shot and I would to cover the area to the left and rear of the dog as a back up.

One by one, very slowly, almost in slow motion at intervals of what seemed like minutes but in fairness was probably long seconds five partridge would launch themselves lightly into the air on the opposite side of the brush and fly toward the open pit.

The first bird merited two shots, one over its head, the second shot ceremonial as the bird was clearly out of range by the time Ernie took it. In some circles this second, meaningless shot is also referred to as a "warning shot".

A second bird emerged and took advantage of the fact that Ernie had not reloaded, believing that the first bird was the lone occupant of the thicket.

"Be ready", I cautioned. "The Grabber's' still birdy, there could be another".

He rolled his eyes, not believing but reloading. He appeared to be ready, tense but not disappointed when the third bird was bumped. This one also hung a right and casually glided away. Once again two spent shotgun shells fell to the gravel road without being accompanied by so much as a single floating tail feather. At this point a growing pile of spent shells was all Ernie had to show for his effort.

After three birds it was no surprise that our shooter was more focused on his failures than his future chances, little possibility that yet another bird could be ready to spring. So no new shells were plopped into his little 20 gauge.

The fourth escaped without so much as a "how do you do" from our man in the field followed almost immediately by the fifth.

"I could shoot myself", he muttered in disgust.

"You know", I mused, "Considering your recent performance I think it would be better if you got someone else to do that for you. You'd probably miss".

Occasionally a display of such diminished shooting skills will trigger a little spontaneous upland hat dance, which is the traditional way of venting frustration over those embarrassing yet inevitable missed shots.

For the uninitiated, hat jumping is sometimes necessitated by the not altogether uncommon missing of a easy shot at a passing woodcock or grouse.

The dance begins by placing one's gun on the ground, followed by throwing your hat next to it. You then leap in rage over both, landing squarely on said hat. All of this normally accompanied by yelling "ratsenfrasenkrat!". Only then is it possible to continue the hunt with some semblance of dignity and decorum.

DOC'S DOGS AND OTHER FOUR LEGGED THOUGHTS

Speaking of embarrassing moments inevitably brings us full circle to dogs.

It's a heavy burden being both an upland bird hunter with a love of snazzy pointing dogs ingrained in every fiber of your being while at the same time to also be a veterinarian. But such was the upland lot in life of my bud Jack.

Naturally, given the breathe of knowledge he so frequently displayed with regard to the medical care and feeding of canines, we expected he would be able to seamlessly blend this expertise with his years of practical bird shooting experiences. This we thought would produce what would no doubt become the finest, flashiest purebred hunting dog ever to be his upland partner in the woods.

Enter Louie Von Bismarck de Human Hund stage left.

We all expected Louie to be the Pointer to End all Pointers but along with Jack were disappointed to discover, that Louie turned out to be little more than a prime candidate for a position as a back-up German parade dog. Louie had no apparent instinct for birdy sports. Birds were not on his radar, not really sure if Louie had any radar.

As friends we were all very careful about offering our opinions on what the matter could be. It's true most guys are kinda insensitive by nature, rather thick skinned by reason of gender, except of course when it comes to their dogs. So we tiptoed around what the matter could be with this fine, handsome (he was cute), expensive upland canine specimen.

First, we postulated that this purebred was a little gun shy, not overtly since he never bolted back to the car or over the horizon when guns were fired. Next, hormones were advanced as an excuse for his seeming lack of attention to the hunting task at hand. He'd play "grab-ass" with all the other dogs regardless of their sexual orientation from the moment we hit our first cover till the end of the day. We became convinced that the dog might not really be a purebred German Short Haired Pointer but rather part "sneaky neighbor's dog".

More importantly, Louie seemed to have no nose for birds. Not sure he could have smelled a woodcock if it were sitting on his nose. Not sure he could have smelled the south end of a north bound skunk for that matter. Jack even tried to train Louie using biscuits and a ball peen hammer.

Finally, after several years of wondering what this dog might be good for the lights went on one crystal clear autumn afternoon in the field behind Henry's Place. We got a look at the Louie in action as he locked on point near a stand of wispy little aspen. Finally, the dog was coming around. What a relief not to have to make sorry excuses about his lack of hunting instinct.

Also, sadly the point was at the bumper of an abandoned Chevy pickup and since the season on pickup bumpers had already closed the first of November not a single shot was fired.

Louie was eventually retired with dignity and returned to the breeder from which he came.

P.S. I've recently been informed that Sam, grown son of Jack has acquired a new bird dog of the German Wire-haired parade dog persuasion. Funny how history has a way of repeating itself.

BEHIND UNITY DUMP
Unity, Maine – Thursday, October 15, 1981

The 1981 Major League Baseball strike began on June 12 and forced the cancellation of 713 games in the middle of the regular season. It cost almost $150 million in lost salaries, ticket sales, broadcast revenues, and concessions.

The owners were unhappy over the issue of the free agency draft, they wanted compensation for the loss of a free agent player to another team.

Begs the Question: If owners were fearful of losing players to free agency... just which Sox players were the Yawkey's afraid of losing?

The woodcock and partridge were not on strike. We went hunting.

Here's what you can expect to get when you decide to ignore your instincts and hunt around a dump. It would be the very last time I would go hunting without a compass.

It turned out that the recycling facility (aka the "dump") in Unity, Maine had a nifty little stand of alders and aspen just down the hillside to the rear of the property.

We'd been directed to this less than pastoral spot by Arnold, who had generously taken it upon himself once again to steer us toward another of his "special" hunting spots. Naturally, as dyed in the wool rubes, it took us several years to realize that his help was more misdirection than direction.

The locals just never tired of making the city boys waste their days in unproductive covers, thus obviously saving the local birds for the local boys.

Willie, Jack and I got to the dump around 2 pm on a brisk and definitively overcast afternoon. We left Jacks' truck on the side of the road about 50 yards from the entrance to the dump and after breaking out both guns and dogs we proceeded down the steep bank behind the dump. It was around 30 feet down to where we were confronted by the edge of a small stream across from which appeared to be some surprisingly decent looking cover.

A few alders were sprinkled around but it was mostly a thin collection of aspen and birch with very thin little ground cover. Even if it proved to be bird-less it would be easy walking and we could be in and out in short order.

Although the murky little stream was too wide to jump, having it spill into your book would quickly turn a pleasant afternoon engaged in the gentlemanly activity of woodcock shooting decidedly unpleasant. We scoped out the stream for twenty yards or so in each direction before finding several strategically placed rocks that would allow for a semi-dry crossing.

The woodcock population that day proved to be generous both in their numbers and in displaying a remarkably cooperative spirit, allowing some among their ranks to be dispatched quickly thereby permitting each of us to end the afternoon just one short of our limit. A still cloud-covered sun was getting low when it got to be time to head back to the truck.

It is at this point that sound judgment, common sense and our collective ability to reason abandoned ship... at least mine and Jack's.

Lacking a visible sun (remember the "definitively overcast day) to give us our bearings as we prepared to trudge back to the truck it turned out that we had no less than three divergent opinions as to the direction we should take. Each opinion would have been separated by about 120 degrees on a compass assuming we had a compass to begin with

Eventually, Jack and I prevailed having negotiated an agreement on a direction that we insisted would take us back to the truck. Sadly, Willie was forced to concur.

Although we didn't consider it strange at the time, we had chosen a direction that did not require that we re-cross the stream that it had been necessary we cross when we first got into the cover.

We even agreed that, no, we had not during the course of our hunting re-crossed the stream, which had that been the case would have made our subsequent decision at least reasonable. Jack and I had simply insisted on a direction to the truck based on intuition. Shaky footing at best.

The next two hours were nasty, sweaty and harrowing, punctuated by a sunset that crept in, followed by total darkness then utter despair. Joining in the depression our dogs stopped hunting taking their clues from the fact that we were wandering aimlessly through what now felt like a jungle, tails between our legs both man and dog.

Several times it became necessary for us to crawl on hands and knees through pine thickets as we hoped upon hope for some sign of civilization which in rural Maine may or may not necessarily be defined as an area inhabited by Mainers.

It was about an hour after all natural light had long since faded that we saw what we thought was the flicker of lights from a farm house some hundred yards across the field the edge of which we had finally stumbled onto. Also, coming into focus was a barn with a shadowy figure, a woman judging from the outline tending to some sort of barn critters. Salvation!

Now we didn't want to startle the farmer so decided to send just one of us on this mission for permission to walk out by way of her house and barn. As I mentioned previously on matters relating to speaking to rural people our default emissary was always Jack the veterinarian. He had that vet way of way of speaking "back country". It was at times like these that we almost expected him to grin and reveal that he too was missing a few front teeth.

So off he went to negotiate our exit as we stayed at the edge of the field tending to the now exhausted dogs and waiting for him to return with permission to walk down the drive to the road out front.

"She has a shotgun" Jack reported on returning. "It was leaning against the barn door. She said 'get the hell out of here' " she won't let us cross her property. She said 'get back in the woods'. Did I mention Jack's ability to connect with the farm folks?

Going back into the woods was clearly not an option so we took our chances with the women with the shotgun. We walked around the edge of her property carefully avoiding her and her barn.

"What if she starts shooting", one of us mused aloud.

"Most likely she'll only have a clear shot at the slowest runner", another offered.

It was a long and still very depressing walk around the perimeter of her fields to the main road and never did the feel of asphalt under foot seem more comforting. But it was still going to be a long, quiet and sobering two mile walk back to the truck even on asphalt. It took us longer than it usually did to find the humor in this one.

On the other hand most locals were amused almost immediately. It did not surprise us that word got around

Unity before sun up the next day about the city boy's adventure at the dump.

It was the buzz at all of Unity's finest breakfast establishments, which almost immediately began offering daily specials featuring "Unity Dumplings".

As a postscript it should be noted that after the retelling of this story on countless occasions my wife finally bought me a hand-held GPS system for my adventures afield. It was more than a little difficult for me to wrap my head around the technology so I ended just not using it. However, once I admitted to that she spirited it away and had it reprogrammed so that now as I'm walking through the alders it periodically says in a wonderful raspy, mechanical voice.

"Don't you think you ought to stop and ask directions?"

FEAR AND LOATHING ON THE MIGHTY MERRIMACK
Or crossing at dawn and other near-death experiences
The Great Marsh, Salisbury, MA - November 10, 1981

Fred Lynn was traded to the California Angles following pre-season opening trades of Butch Hobson and Rick Burleson. I just had a bad feeling all year long about this one.

We finished an ignominious (i.e. marked by shame) 5th place.

Had a similar bad feeling about what turned out to be my last duck hunt on the Merrimack.

The Merrimack River where we frequently went duck hunting back in the 70's and 80's used to be awash with migratory waterfowl as they sped along the Atlantic flyway;

black ducks, mallards, teal and the occasional canvasback were all drawn irresistibly to the seclusion of the expansive wetlands known as the Salisbury marshes. The flocks were at times so large that when they banked, turning in unison it would nearly create an eclipse of the early morning sun.

The marshes where we hunted were tough to get to, for all practical purposes not a walk-in. The most sensible approach was approach by boat necessitating a crossing of the menacingly swift and unforgiving Merrimack River from the Newburyport side. One of the better

areas to set up blinds was maybe a couple of miles in from the open ocean in a backwater subject to the rise and fall of six foot or so tides. The tides had sufficient flushing capacity when outgoing to give fits and starts to even decent sized Boston Whalers sporting 40 plus out or inboards. Hunting the Salisbury marshes meant arriving early to pick your spot.

Once in place you needed to be committed to stay with your chosen spot for the duration of the hunt. These marshes were a patch work of pliable earth, in a continuous pre-muckian stage crisscrossed by tidal channels that are about a foot and a half too wide to jump over. Too wide to vault for us but not wide enough to cause a blip in the stride of, say an energetic lab rushing to retrieve a downed teal. So moving your blind was neither desirable nor practical. Let the dog do the work.

On the morning in question our rig consisted of a 3 hp Johnson c.1954 mounted on a small aluminum row boat with loose rivets.

We loaded the boat with a 50 or so pound bag of Mr. Bean's finest decoys and 120 pounds of Willie's finest black Labrador retriever, The Grabber. It seemed a perfectly safe and seaworthy craft fitted with a perfectly safe and seaworthy cargo, especially if your brain was still operating in a typical sleep deprived, up too early kind of way.

The Grabber

Oh yeah, on this particular day we also tossed in three hunters with combined middle aged girths that bumped up the load another 675 or so pounds in addition to the gear.

The morning was dim and chilly with a little drizzle thrown in just to underscore the fact that it was 5:15 am and none of us had gotten through our first cup of coffee. Did I mention that the river was choppy, accented by nasty little swirling eddies along with a slight but tenacious breeze of 10 to 15 mph? Our ever optimistic objective: the Salisbury marshes for an early morning encounter with, we hoped, some blacks, mallards or perhaps a chubby little Canvasback.

As we began crossing the river, I noted through bleary eyes that the rocking, pitching motion of the bow and stern was growing more and more pronounced. Then about half way across the river and without any warning the bow went under and we swamped. Our instinctive reaction... we stood up! We were, however, already submerged to the gunnels, fortunately the flotation built into the seats managing to keep us from actually going to the bottom.

From the shore it must have looked like three hunters walking to the marshes.

Magically, our rugged little 3 horse Johnson continued to putt away and push us from the middle of the river toward safety and the marshy but drier shore.

I had managed to grab the decoy bag and each of us had grabbed our respective guns. The immediate casualties of the dunking were a spare gas can, which floated away, soaked rears ends and our oars which were rapidly heading out to sea in the outgoing rip. The Grabber, our black lab companion had abandoned ship and was busy making it to the marsh.

This was among the longest two to three minutes of my life which passed by like an out-of-body experience until our swamped rig made the shore of the marsh. For reasons I never quite understood we still decided to set up for some shooting.

The unanswered question for the ages of course was: If our boat was still motoring,

When bottom and river bottom meet

and we were half way across the river, why not just turn around and head back where the warmth of hearth and home would allow us to leave this tragic hunt behind, behind?

94

But, as has been proven time after time to be a universal truth, men in small swamped aluminum boats are slow learners.

It was only in the last forty yards of our approach that we noticed a hunter already set up and hunkered down in a meticulously constructed reed blind, his rather classy looking Chesapeake Retriever peering at us over the top of the marsh grass, his rather classy looking duck boat tucked neatly away at the head of the adjacent channel.

He was dressed in tweeds, of the stuffy English hunting variety, a sure sign of trouble to come.

Unfortunately, he also noticed us. I supposed it would be hard not to notice three guys standing in a boat full of water, motor running, all three clutching decoys, guns and other paraphernalia as they are being guided through the marsh by a large, black lab too embarrassed to get back in the boat with us, thus deciding to swim along in front.

Awkwardly, we apologized as we chugged by for the intrusive, late, noisy, unorthodox arrival. His wave said "no problem" but his irritation with our disruptive entrance was written all over his face.

A boat full of the Merrimack River

Naturally, given our circumstance setting up for the hunt took a little longer than usual. We needed to pull the boat and empty it, all the while listening to Willie complain about the soaking the seat of his pants took. Meantime, our marsh neighbor's patience with our intrusion seem to grow even thinner.

The Grabber spent most of the first half hour visiting the other hunter's blind, presumably begging to be adopted much to the chagrin of the Chessy who had begrudgingly made room for him in their blind.

When we called The Grabber he wouldn't even look at us, still too embarrassed by our jackass moves in the river to be seen with us for the balance of the morning.

Soon enough we got down to the serious business of duck shooting. It wasn't too long before a couple of mallards settled into our decoy set. Jack was the first up and brought one down before it had gotten ten feet off the water.

The tide, however, immediately began sweeping the mallard downstream where if not retrieved quickly it would join our errant oars and gas can which were probably already in open ocean. The Grabber continued to stubbornly ignore Willie's call to retrieve the bird so having no choice Jack sprang into action. He jumped in the boat and gave chase in an effort to retrieve the duck himself. Off he went around the bend in the inlet stream putt by putt by putt.

About ten minutes later Willie and I exchanged the first of what would become a number of puzzled looks. Since we were helplessly abandoned in the marsh with no way out and no means of launching an attempt to rescue Jack we decided to adopt a wait and see attitude.

Having resolved that philosophy, no action was the only tool at our disposal, we shrugged and scanned the skyline for incoming canards.

Several more minutes passed when at last we saw the bow of the boat begin to creep around the bend, hugging the opposite bank of the inlet. First the bow, then mid-ship, then Jack in the stern grasping at marsh grass hand-over-hand to pull the little boat upstream. He'd run out of gas on his way back so his return to the blind necessitated both pulling the boat along the shore and paddling with the stock of his shotgun which he'd brought along in case the mallard had just been clipped.

Let's review. Here we are about 150 yards from safety and the warm embrace of civilization across the Merrimack River in an isolated swamp, facing an outgoing tide with more than three hours to go before it would turn in our favor, no gas, and we're set up near an increasingly hostile hunter whom we'd just irritated again.

After considerable discussion about the possibility of paddling across the river even with three shotgun stocks working simultaneously it was clear that we really had only one... albeit distasteful option.

We needed to ask our marsh neighbor if we could borrow a cup of gas.

Now, finding straws of either the long or short variety in a marsh that we could draw in order to determine who was going to ask for this momentous favor was no problem.

Lots of straw around.

So, Jack, who from that moment on known would become known as Jack of the short straw, reluctantly paddled down the twenty or so yards to the guy's blind to beg for a little petrol. You'd like to think that the best of human nature prevailed. You'd like to think that. But even with Jack pleading for mercy, even with sniveling, groveling and whining only one deal could be struck. Our marsh companion would provide the gas provided we agreed to leave.

Secretly, I applauded his tenacity in sticking to this requirement. It was actually not such a bad deal considering the wonderful time we'd had so far.

This hunting experience immediately gave rise to the founding of the Greater Newburyport Breakfast Sipping & Shooting Society. Its' charter members committed to embracing a more civilized, sane approach to achieving camaraderie than duck hunting could ever provide.

Members focused, having previously scouted out the best breakfast establishments in the area, on closing duck blinds early, or foregoing them entirely to retire to a short stack with bacon and talking about bygone hunts.

SALAD DAYS & ANDROSCOGGIN NIGHTS
Errol, New Hampshire – May 15, 16, 17, 1982

Even with the addition of free agent Mark "the bird" Fidrych we could only manage a third place finish behind the Orioles and still hot Brewers.

This was Ralph Houk's second year managing the team and for the second season had helped the team make things interesting. The Milwaukee Brewer however made things even more interesting with a first place 95 and 67 record, just a game ahead of the Orioles.

Regulars on the hill in '82 were Bob Stanley, John Tudor, Mark Clear, Mike Torrez and the Eck. Carney Lansford held down third until the introduction of a rookie named

Wade Boggs who latched onto the position when Lansford was injured in June and never let go finishing the season with an eye catching .349 average.

In those carefree post-Ossipee, post-winning days we decided to try our hands and hooks on the big river.

If you've never fished the Androscoggin it's unlikely you'll be able to appreciate the near-death experience that every wader has when encountering its moss covered bottom.

The well-known malady that befalls anglers who venture into such vertically challenging waters… is called the "stumble f**ks making wading sticks a necessity.

A wading stick, however is more likely to only end up assisting people along the river bank in seeing you as you are swept by flailing it helplessly in the air, on your one way trip to the pulp mincing machine at the Brown Paper Company in

Berlin only to make your final earthly appearance as a part of the Sports Section of the New York Sunday Times.

In such treacherous waters almost every other kind of activity provides a welcome diversion from the monumental task of actually catching fish in these near unfishable waters.

Activities for instance like shopping for advice or trout flies at locally famous Brown Owl Cabins and Fly Fisherman Rip-Off Emporium.

The owner of the establishment, Bob thenceforth became known as Bobby Brown Owl, a name which when uttered amongst my little group still produces head shaking accompanied by eye rolling.

"So Bobby, what are they hitting?" we would query. His answer would soon become known as the Androscoggin quick step.

A glance at his fly case made predicting "what they're hitting" a sure bet. What they were hitting would be whatever there were the most of left unsold in the case. These would become the recommendation of the day.

"Muddlers", he would intone with a smarmy sincerity and solemnity honed razor sharp through a lifetime of experience sucking the wallets of hapless fisher people dry.

Ok then, muddlers it would be and we would stock up on muddlers for the days piscatorial hunt. Of course when we returned later that day complaining that the recommended selection attracted not a single rise the response was always the same "You should have been here yesterday".

Thereafter, whenever we asked any local to recommend a fly pattern that seemed to be working, we framed the question a little differently.

"We had planned to arrive tomorrow so we'd appreciate it if you could tell us what might work then so we can use it today." Even extensive planning is no substitute for common sense.

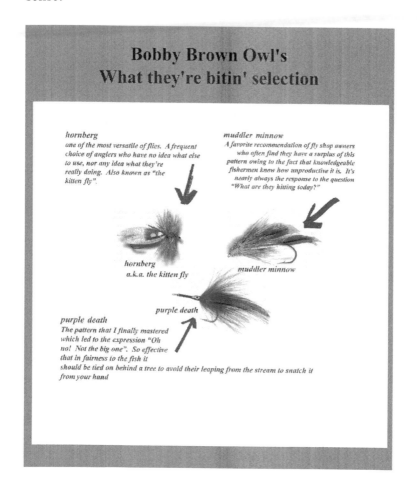

Bobby Brown Owl's
What they're bitin' selection

hornberg
one of the most versatile of flies. A frequent choice of anglers who have no idea what else to use, nor any idea what they're really doing. Also known as "the kitten fly".

muddler minnow
A favorite recommendation of fly shop owners who often find they have a surplus of this pattern owing to the fact that knowledgeable fishermen know how unproductive it is. It's nearly always the response to the question "What are they hitting today?"

hornberg
a.k.a. the kitten fly

muddler minnow

purple death

purple death
The pattern that I finally mastered which led to the expression "Oh no! Not the big one". So effective that in fairness to the fish it should be tied on behind a tree to avoid their leaping from the stream to snatch it from your hand

Planning for our annual fishing extravaganza to the Androscoggin River up around Errol, NH was a firmly established ritual which was carried out in early March over a couple of ice cold Narragansett's and pizza at the Park Lunch. Yes, the very same Park Lunch where we hatched our plans for trips to Ossipee.

Years of experience, however, had taught us that throwing a couple of pup tents, the big skillet and a canteen or two of bourbon into the truck just wouldn't do. A little rain and a swarm of black flies could mess up a weekend in a hurry.

This year, the year in question would be different. In addition to our standard packing list which included the staples of Oreos, Cheese Doodles, and Italian hot peppers, this year we were bringing a dining tent. Damn near high society!

We arrived brimming with optimism in the belief that surely this time the planets would be aligned in our favor. A sure sign from the gods that we had to swerve only once to avoid a bull moose not more than two hundred yards from our campsite. Moose sightings were considered to be an omen of good things and good times to come.

We did not, however, arrive with any measure of common sense, most of us having left that behind at birth.

In picking the spot to set up our gear, we had chosen a slightly flattened out, inviting little piece of ground at the base of the fifty yard long dirt access road that led down from the "tar" road. Pitching our tents here, we reasoned would put us next to the river and provide ready access in and out.

Sadly, the dirt road would also provide easy access for other things as well. Like a torrent of rushing rain water making a bee line to the river as water is traditionally inclined to do by following the gravitational path of least resistance. A dirt road free of undergrowth and most other forest floor debris is the rural definition of least resistance.

As you might expect it rained rather torrentially that evening so we spent our oblivious post dinner hours in the dining tent, Coleman lanterns blazing, poker chips flying, snack-a-tizers (the camping equivalent of appetizers) all around, smug in the knowledge that we seemed to have beaten the fickle fishing god odds by avoiding an old fashioned soaking. We were sure that the morrow would bring big fish and bigger stories.

Now, tradition on these outings demanded that everyone had a responsibility to consume an appropriate amount of what had come to be known as the "brown stuff" (aka bourbon) and this night would be no exception. We spent several hours meeting that obligation while at the same time entertaining each other by trying out what were a few pretty good impressions of Steve Martin and Dan Aykroyd, as "two wild and crazy guys". Juvenile to be sure… Funny? …you had to be there.

Eventually, the soothing rhythms of big yawns in syncopation filled the drizzly evening air. It was bedtime and still raining. Ben had been slumped over a bag of Oreo crumbs for about an hour when someone observed that perhaps we should check his pulse.

This gave rise to one of our favorite guys-away-for-the-weekend mantras. Not really wanting to expend the energy to struggle to my feet and actually go over to Ben to check on his well being I opined "Ya know if he's dead now, he'll be dead in the morning". The nice part about this truism is that it applies equally well to those who have merely passed out as well as those who have passed on.

Taking mercy, however we shook him, woke him and suggested it might be time for him to retire. A little groggy he stumbled to his feet and saw the rain that was pouring down. You could almost see him contemplating the possibility that having consumed a little too much brown stuff might give rise to problems later on.

That in mind he wisely decided that he should bring a pot to bed in case his dinner decided to make an unannounced middle-of-the-night reappearance. He could, he reasoned, thereby avoid getting up and going out into the rainy night. Fill pot if necessary, empty pot in morning went the logic.

By dawn the rain had in fact let up to make room for heavy grey skies. We were rather rudely confronted with the aftermath that any rain bestows on campers; that of a sopping wet campsite. You know the drill, unwashed dishes from the night before, mud and muck at every footfall, no cozy campfire and no possibility of or enthusiasm for starting one.

Not to mention the reality of our tent having been pitched right in the middle of the dirt road, better known as the "stream bed", leading down to and through our site. The same road which was poised to become a gully in the right weather, did so. In fact, the remnants of a small stream still trickled through the center of the tent finding its way under our sleeping bags only to emerge on the low side and continue to trickle on down to the river. This was Ben's tent of "take a pot to bed" fame.

He emerged, unshaven, stinky and looking every bit like the victim of a midnight mugging. Funny thing about Ben is that he looked the same way when we picked him up to begin the trip as when we dropped him off. It was almost as if he took a couple of days off in advance to drink, not shave and sleep in his clothes.

"Ben?" we queried, "little wet in there?"

"%#$+@", he replied.

"End up needing that pot last night?"

"Yeah, but it wasn't a pot. It was a colander".

A SHORT BUT INSTRUCTIVE TREATISE ON THE UNSUNG MEDICINAL QUALITIES OF BOURBON

On the heels of our encounter with the colander we found it wise to revisit the positive medicinal qualities of the liquid that contributed to this man versus. pot confrontation.

It is fall in New England. It is time to start the pre-hunting season discussion. Old equipment, old memories, old friends, old bourbon and fresh hopes emerge. Bourbon, having nothing whatsoever to do technically with the hunting of woodcock or in the fishing for trout often receives short shrift in even the more complete treatises on this subject.

This oversight is but one of the many examples of the neglect and glossing of the subject which compelled me to re-confront the subject leading with my best shot.

Understanding the importance of bourbon to the addicted woodcock aficionado misses the point, not unlike the result when most of us take aim on the little critter; that is missing the shot. For without bourbon what would be the elixir that would instigate the exaggerations and hyperbole which are the lifeblood of our discussions of epic timber doodle hunts past, present and future?

What sour mash substitute would allow a marginally successful hunt to be transported days later to a place where visions of limits shot, unfailing aim and perfect points from every puppy abound? In truth vodka, gin and a variety of other stuff will also turn the trick… but that's beside the point.

One time, over a social bourbon at Henry's place in Unity, one of his friends, an old Mainer told us that if you watched carefully you could see a woodcock lean just before it took flight; leaning right if it was to fly to the right, left if… and so on. This bald faced exaggeration can actually be embraced as fact given the proper amount of lubricant imbibed before it's telling.

We have on file an affidavit from a Mr. Bert Calder of Bangor who on trooping through a particularly soggy alder run accidentally planted his gun snoot first in the mud. A quick rub with a bourbon soaked cloth restored the sheen immediately, though it so distracted his attention thereafter on mounting the gun as to compromise an otherwise perfect outing.

The parallels between woodcock and a little Tennessee lightning abound. The woodcock is a warm little beastie, as is bourbon.

Unlike bourbon, however the wily woodcock won't stay with you for very long unless it is detained. By contrast, I have personally had bourbon or a very strong memory of it stay with me well beyond noon of the following day.

Both of them have nicknames. The woodcock is best known as a timber doodle, while bourbon has been appropriately saddled with the less flattering moniker "loud mouth soup" It should be noted that gin and vodka are close cousins to bourbon and are frequently substituted straight over ice and garnished with olives and lemon twists, know as a martini or "crystal yum-yum"

Both elicit fond memories, memories which incidentally are always better than the realities upon which the initial experiences were based.

Oh yeah! The medicinal qualities? They're both good for you, making you at one and the same time both louder and funnier.

They say laughter is the best medicine.

YET ANOTHER ANDROSCOGGIN EVENING
Errol, New Hampshire – June 2, 3, 4, 1982

Will someone please put the Red Sox out of my misery?

Notwithstanding our ill-fated attempt to beat the effects of rain and a black fly attack that made even the ugliest locust plague look like a walk in the park we decided to return again to the scene of our crimes. Once again we were proven to be slow learners.

It would be just a short year later that with the dining tent in hand we were back at the Androscoggin.

It would also be the last time any of us tried to combine fishing and camping thinking the result would be a good time. This outing later became known as the Greater Androscoggin Building Permit Caper.

Arriving on a Thursday afternoon around three we were welcomed by the a few sprinkles of rain gently splattering our windshields. The forecast was for more of the same later that evening but a sunny weekend was in sight.

Undaunted, we broke out fly rods, waders, Muddler Minnows and headed for the river. What, after all, is a little rain? Well, a little rain on a camping trip, for those among you who are not as clear as you should be about it, is similar to a Chinese water torture, especially after about three or so hours looking out from under a dripping hat brim punctuated by the clammy fingers that accompany most early May rains.

We had split into two groups for our first try at the river. Group one… (Jack, Hank and I) preferred the large pool below the Errol Dam while the others opted for an equally treacherous piece of the river further downstream After a couple of fishless hours, we packed it in heading back to camp, soaked and ready to sop up a bit of our beloved liquid entertainment.

The boys from group two had already arrived and were making an effort to get a fire started. Ben, under the supervision of Éclair Eddie, was fanning a smoldering pile of "not fire" at his feet.

Éclair Eddie had earned this nickname on a previous excursion by showing superhuman restraint, saving, unbeknownst to the rest of us, a box of those chocolaty treats for the last night of a three night trip. Needless to say this was much to the amazement and delight of all.

It was apparent that there were no ex-Boy Scouts in that Group Two since what seemed to be emanating from the little pile of small twigs and wet leaves that had been assembled was an agitated spiraling plume of thick white smoke, determined to choke out any flames that might try to emerge.

Once we re-focused and could see beyond the smoke the real evidence of Group Two's ineptitude was apparent. Strung over the fire and clearing it by about two feet was a lawn chair, its bent aluminum structure suspended by ropes running in three or four directions to nearby trees (nearby being on at least one leg of the architecture about 15 feet). The idea was to protect the struggling fire from the continuing drizzle by shielding, umbrella-like with the chair.

These were the kind of lawn chairs that featured that now instantly recognizable and quite nifty 60's multi-colored woven plastic fabric we've all come to admire.

The fabric was not so much combustible as it was melt-able. Ironically, if this effort to provide a canopy somehow miraculously worked and fire was the result it was still sure to end tragically for the unwitting piece of lawn furniture.

Have I already mentioned that Hank, a founding member of our group was by trade a cabinetmaker of the first order?

Along with the skill with woodworking tools that profession demands he was further imbued with a knack for fixing almost anything.

Once, while we were musing about really deep issues around a poker table the question of what you'd want to have in the event you were deserted on the proverbial dessert island the group unanimously concurred. You'd want a Hank, handier than a dozen Swiss Army knives, able to resurrect our infamous little 3 horse Johnson after years of disuse and misuse using a screwdriver and a rock, able to leap...

So after our initial shock Hank kicked into high gear.

"Where's that big tarp we brought?" he said, taking command.

Within minutes he had also located not only the tarp but a 50 yard coil of clothesline, a rather handy little tree saw and one dull hatchet. More than enough tools to both begin and complete the project which he started by felling five small trees with trunk diameters in the 5 to 6 inch range. These became the corner posts and center post of a tent which would he would erect over the fire and campers for the duration of the storm.

In due course the tarp-tent took shape and the center pole which was roughly ten feet long was pushed into place, coaxing the tarp into the shape of a poorly designed circus big top.

Now we'd get that pesky fire stared and begin drying out.

Thus commenced one of the most uncomfortable camping evenings any of us can recall. Yes, the fire after not too long a time began to show life, then more life...then even more. In fact that little pile of (still wet) leaves, sticks and small logs was becoming quite capable of going through the night. It seemed determined however to continue to throw off just as much smoke as heat.

Among the design flaws in the tarp-tent was a lack of ventilation at its peak. The Indians had figured it out hundreds if not thousands of years ago. Tepees were laid up with a ventilating hole at the peak... TO LET THE SMOKE OUT!

Our design engineer was apparently unwilling to adopt this time honored technique so it wasn't too long before the tarp-tent/rain shelter began to fill with thick, acrid smoke.

Still, you'd think a ten foot vertical center clearance might have been sufficient until you discovered that the accumulating smoke filled at least four to five feet with no chance of escaping into the evening air.

This left about five feet of untainted air in which we could congregate, re-tell old fishing stories and be miserable. All of us are taller than five feet.

A second design flaw was that the lower edges of the tarp sagged creating handy pouches in which rain water running down could collect. To avoid inhaling smoke all evening the five of us had to stand around the campfire hunched over, Quasimodo like, periodically stepping out from under the shelter of the tarp-tent into the pouring rain to avoid asphyxiation. Each time anyone stepped away from the shelter of the tarp-tent they would bump the tent causing the pooled rainwater to rush immediately down their neck.

Life is good if not just a little smoky from time to time.

OH HOW GOOD IT IS TO FEEL LIKE YOU'RE TWELVE AGAIN ... *(and embarrassing)*
West Kennebec, Maine – Friday, October 15, 1982

Red Sox dropped another one to the Orioles 2-5 today.

This had been a lackluster season even with the team playing ten games over 500 to this point. It was a rookie named Wade Boggs' major league debut. He went 0 for 4.

To my never ending frustration Boggs seemed incapable of swinging at a first pitch. He did however manage to accumulate more than 3000 hits. Superstitious by nature Boggs attributed his success to a carefully followed ritual preceding every game. It began with chowing down on chicken, ergo the clubhouse nickname "Chicken Man".

He won the AL batting title five times, staying with the Sox through the '92 season and finished with an average of .338. Only Teddy finished higher.

He entered the hallowed halls at Cooperstown in 2005.

After hunting Howard's place for four or five seasons something remarkable happened. It turned out to be one of the best days of all my days afield.

Willie and I pulled up to Howard's place in the usual manner, parking under the big old maple. Howard came out and we commenced with a discussion of the weather.

"Awfully dry this year, Howard.", I said belaboring the obvious.

"Yessah", he kicked a stone in the drive. "Dry."
Howard was a man of few words in case you didn't notice.

113

"Not a lot of pa'tridge. Too dry." he continued. I believed him, not good news but after all, who knew the state grouse populations at the Howards place better than the man his own self.

I'm not exactly sure how the dry conditions contributed since grouse didn't migrate and the drought had been pretty much an all east coast affair.

But then, just as I was about to seek clarification, Howard abruptly announced that he wanted to go hunting with us that morning. He wanted to show us a couple of his "special" spots. Think about it! All mention of the paucity of pa'tridge was gone.

He was willing to take time from his busy schedule of watching the winter rye grow to spend a little quality time with his adopted "boys". It doesn't get any better than this!

The three of us would have been a sight to behold. Willie and I, of course were perfectly attired in the latest in hunter orange vests and other snappy upland apparel from L.L.

Whatever… No such sartorial splendor for Howard. He simply stepped back inside the kitchen door grabbed an ancient 16 gauge, adjusted the brim of his cap, hiked up his overalls and was ready to go.

It wasn't until we got to the first "special" spot that we discovered that Howard hadn't brought any shells. This was not accidental. He didn't mean to. That's when it dawned on me that he never had any intention of shooting.

He just wanted to be with us. He was taking the "boys" hunting sort of the way my dad did when I was twelve and we went on a squirrel shoot. Dad carried a 410 gauge although he never put a shell in it, and I a slingshot. For that matter neither did I until I turned ten and he became convinced that me and a loaded shotgun represented no risk to either of us.

There we were at the first "special" spot which was only about a half mile from his house over where the tar road gave way to gravel. The cover consisted of a five or six acre field at the end of which was a patch of alders swaying and beckoning in the breeze for us to come on in. A veritable woodcock hotel as they say.

Well, Howard could show up with no shells if he wanted, but I was a veritable arsenal of 20 gauge low brass 7 ½'s. I slipped a couple into my favorite over and under, checked the safety and then released the then, nearly levitating with excitement English Setter Ike, free from the confines of his kennel.

The guys I hunted with thought for the longest time that his name was actually "No-Ike" since that was what I always seemed to be saying to him. He leaped from the tailgate, ready to hunt, turned abruptly ran ten paces and locked solidly on point at the side of the road.

Now that was convenient. This spot really was special. I looked at Willie, still pulling his gun from its case, not ready to take a shot.
I looked at "No Shells" Howard. He grinned and motioned toward the dog with a boney index finger, indicating that I

should go ahead and do the honors. And take the shot I would. I slipped in quietly behind Ike, encouraging him to hold his point.

"Steady up, steady…" Ike had the courtesy to hold his point and resist his deepest urge to bust the bird thereby not embarrassing me in front of Howard.

Then I carefully nudged past him to see if I could flush the bird. I was surrounded by a full 270 degrees of open air and a clear line of sight. Very little was there to obstruct a clean shot surrounding the spot where the bird was most likely sitting. I figured the bird's only hope would be if it headed immediately toward the trucks open tailgate seeking refuge in the vehicles back seat. Otherwise, I figured this was one woodcock destined to spend the night with a package of frozen peas.

Yes, this was indeed a special spot. This was indeed a special moment. This was indeed a time I would never forget. But for the wrong reasons.

Heart pounding, both the bird's no doubt and mine, the doodle launched and took off at what seemed like breakneck speed. Flying straight away into the open and nearly level at about 5 feet, the woodcock was headed directly down the gravel road.

This would be easy. If we were out on the links this would have been a "gimmie putt".

BAM! Not even a puff of tail feathers.

BAM!

The second shot merely ceremonial, one not really fired with enthusiasm nor with the expectation that a fallen bird would be the result. And in this case the result was in fact a woodcock well launched on it's way to bask in the winter suns of Louisiana.

Now came the true test of my character… turning around to face Willie and more importantly Howard feeling every bit like the twelve year old he had taken to his special spot. I fully expected, "Nice try kid. I think I might have had some trouble hitting that one."

Thankfully, both had already turned away and were examining the toes of their shoes as if they hadn't noticed a thing.

BOSEBUCK, RANGELEY AND THE DOCTOR'S KITTEN
Wilson Mills, Maine – June 1984

The '84 season produced a fourth place finish. Yikes! At least we had Clemens and Eckersley and featured in the side show there was always Oil Can Boyd.

Life around Fenway is never dull.

We discovered the camps at Bosebuck accidentally. Willie came up with the idea to try randomly. We had tired of the trip to Unity. Henry's place had been reduced to a pile of ashes and staying at the Unity No Tell Motel just didn't make it for us.

So we were adrift with no where to go and began to flail about aimlessly looking for new fertile grounds to hunt.

But it was a little like playing Pin-the-Tail-on-the-Hunting-Camp... blindfolded, big map, spin and stick a pin. Bingo we're going to Bosebuck. It turned out to be a pretty good accidental find and we kept it going for several years. Bosebuck Mountain Camps is located about 14 miles down a dusty logging road on the western shore of Aziscohos Lake which you reach about 20 miles down Rt.16 west of Rangeley, Maine where you bang a right in Wilson's Mills.

The place is a turn-of-some-century old lake-side hunting and fishing retreat down what had once been a logging road running in and out of some big paper company's logging operation. It features small, one room log cabins sprinkled all over the camp near the edge of Aziscohos.

The camp at the time we discovered it was run by Jack and Susan Rideout, a couple of rugged individualists who were committed to making what I'm sure was a pretty gritty living out of pointing city slicks in the direction of the occasional trout, salmon, woodcock or grouse. Since these outings were not infrequently pretty unproductive owing chiefly to the lack of skill of their guests in upland pursuits they wisely added value to the stay by serving fancy meals featuring the likes of lobster and steak. The evening meal was always served on white linen tablecloths in the dining room of a salty main lodge which could have been a stage set for a turn of century lodge.

The lodge featured a moose-headed fireplace and knotty pine walls festooned with pictures of smiling turn-of-the-century sporting ladies in the sporting lady attire of the day holding stringers of not so smiley landlocked salmon the sizes of which having not been taken from that lake or any other in about a century.

No doubt among those earliest anglers to wet a line on Aziscohos, Magalloway and Parmachenee rivers would have been Maine's very own Cornelia "Fly Rod" Crosby, renowned in the Rangeley Lakes area for her fishing prowess and the fact that she was granted the first Maine Guide license in 1897, man or woman.

That's the kind of place Bosebuck was, reeking of history from every pore..

Jack and I had planned a three-day trip for trout at Bosebuck.

Cornelia "Fly Rod" Crosby

To get a jump on it we decided to drive up the night before and stay in Errol, New Hampshire signature accommodations, the no star Errol Motel. That way we could get an early start to Bosebuck arriving just before mid-morning.

I was to drive to Jack's before dinner, load my gear in his Trooper, leave my car in the driveway then we'd make an after-dark escape for a long weekend of fishing. The only minor wrench in the works were sheets of rain and the prospect of a grueling, pitch black drive up along the Androscoggin featuring limited visibility all the way.

Our last trip up that country road had almost ended in a twisted pile of J.C., Jack, Jack's Trooper and a moose.

Somewhere along the 13 mile woods a big one bounded out unannounced from the darkness at the side of the road and came across right in front of the Trooper.

We came so close to the moose that Jack, ever the veterinarian observed that if his window had been down he would have been close enough to have given the big guy a prostate exam as he ran across the road.

But I'm getting ahead of my self. We'd been on the road from Jack's house for about an hour and had begun searching in the still pouring rain for a place to grab a bite.

Since only traditional fishing trip fare will do on a fishing trip magically; almost mystically a spotlight lit sign announcing "World Famous Dogs." Jack eased the Trooper over peering through the fog and drizzle of the night, making a hard right into the parking lot and we both made a dash to the take-out window to grab a couple of dogs with the works.

It's hard to imagine anything better than the heater blowing hot and steamy on a cold at drizzly night while you're about to chow down on a couple of steamy dogs slathered with relish, mustard and kraut. It was the perfect buffer against that rainy evening. It's hard to imagine anything better but you know what's impossible to image?

Your fishing buddy dropping said SUV into reverse as we're beginning to pull away from World Famous Hot Dogs and continue the drive when suddenly he slams on the brakes throws it in park, leaps out of the truck and begins chasing a kitten around the parking lot.

Turned out the kitten was in fact his family's newest pet who had somehow managed to stowaway undetected for the entire

60 or so mile trip from Exeter to Ossipee. One entire side of the kitten was soaking wet, nose to tail, the other dry as a bone. Apparently the kitten had climbed into the engine compartment in an effort to stay dry while Jack's SUV was parked in his driveway.

Seems the kitten had no other place to stay dry and warm while waiting for someone let it back into the house. You can imagine its surprise when the old hunt mobile sprang to life and began to move his cozy little shelter out of the driveway and down the road.

Once Jack finally cornered, then finally captured the little guy, my immediate suggestion was to inquire as to the hot dog stand waitress's willingness to adopt. A suggestion I would add that was summarily dismissed. I still don't understand since it's not like a vet would have a whole lot of trouble getting a replacement kitten. Thus began the weekend of a couple of hard drinking, outdoorsy hunting, fishing buddies and their fluffy little white kitten.

Our pit stop the next morning for gas drew more than a few incredulous stares at the kitten sitting in plain view on the dashboard but the bizarre animal weekend was really just begging.

The road into Bosebuck is long, dusty and normally uninhabited by any living thing other than the occasional pa'tridge crossing the road. (To get to the other side) We had just checked our way in at the Wilson Mills entry gate and driven no more than about two miles when we noticed two yellow tail tiger butterflies sitting in the road, you know the large bright yellow and black ones. I remarked that they were a relatively rare species and it was unusual to see two at the same time. (Yeah, we were talking about butterflies)

On cue, around the next bend sitting in the road were about a half dozen of these "rare" butterflies. Needless to say this extraordinary sighting did not pass without comment.

"Jeez", I astutely remarked. "Look at that".

Over the next two or three miles these "rare" butterflies covered the road in groups by the tens if not hundreds. Butterflies... kittens...

So when we arrived at Bosebuck just before noon we decided to park Jack's SUV as far from our fellow sportsmen as possible in an effort to keep our adorable little kitten out of the limelight.

We checked in and got our cabin assignment then wandered over to begin unpacking our gear. The cabin was no more than ten or fifteen feet from the edge of Aziscohos where a twelve foot aluminum pram was pulled partially up the bank. I walked over to take a look at the boat and peruse the lake when I noticed a rope like object right in front of the boat.

Thamnophis sirtalis!!!

A garter snake somewhere in the vicinity of a foot plus in length was coiled up right in front of the boat.

I'm not, nor is Jack in the least bothered by snakes. At least not the varieties commonly encountered in our corner of New England. Not the first time I've bumped into one of these critters. Normally you can move them along with a shuffle of you foot in their direction, or a more aggressive kick that produces some dirt flying toward them.

Not this fellow. He dug in, tightened his coil and refused to move. In fact he gave us a little attitude. Even a couple of nudges with a long stick failed to convince him of the futility of his cause. I conceded the territory to him and returned to check out our cabin.

After we had unpacked we spent a long afternoon on the Upper Magalloway, small kitten frolicking in the back of the truck at stream side. Darn cute kitten by the way.

So far though, we'd managed to keep our manly reputations at least temporarily intact.

Evening fell, dinner was uneventful, our cabin was inviting.

About 6 am; earlier than it was our habit to rise we were stirred by a voice accompanied by a knock on our cabin door.

"Doc?" someone tentatively inquired.

"Jack," I said…"it's for you".

"Doc" the voice persisted "Sorry to bother you but your kitten has a fly in its mouth"

the "kitten" fly

Seems fluffy had been playing with our still strung fly rods in the back of the truck and managed to get a hornberg tucked firmly into her upper lip. She'd been prancing around the truck jumping from front to back seat in an effort to rid herself of the fly and was noticed by a passing member of the kitchen crew. Curses! The kitten was out of the bag.

Our surgeon went to work and in short order the kitten was once again fly-less and we were able to return to the serious business of fishing. To help restore our manly reputations we would end up spending the balance of our trip spitting, adjusting our crotches and talking to everybody we came into contact with about football.

After breakfast that morning, where we were convinced that everyone in the dining room was holding back snickers, we asked Tom Rideout where he thought we ought to spend the morning.

Here again we had naively repeated what has proven to be one of the two most consistent mistakes in judgment that slicks make … ask a local where to fish.

Nevertheless, we asked our host where a good, secluded place might be to flex a fly rod or two. He said there was a private, remote brookie spot on the inlet stream to the Parmachenee, the long narrow lake that was connected to the Aziscohos by the Upper Magalloway. He suggested that it just might be just the ticket. We than were told that the Parmachenee could be "easily" accessed by Bosebuck guests.

Specifically, the spot in question was known as "Little Boy Falls". You could "easily" get there by driving to the first locked gate several miles north of camp, then we could "easily" carry canoe paddles and a can of gas to fuel the little 3hp on the Bosebuck canoe that was tethered at lakeside.

This "easy" hike in, of course would also include carrying fly rods, vests, rain gear and a Bosebuck bagged lunch which for some reason always contained a green apple hard enough to drive a ten penny nail. All of which was to be accomplished wearing a pair of heavy duty, sweat inducing Red Ball waders in which if history is a reliable guide there would soon appear an untimely rip in the crotch..

Anyway his suggestion seemed reasonable to us so after making sure our kitten was secure in the back of Jack's SUV we headed down, loaded to the gills with stuff to find the canoe and discover this new "secret" place.

Stuff in hand, we found the canoe and fifteen minutes later we were putting over the Parmachenee. The Parmachenee shoreline was pristine; no dwellings, no imprint of man's presence now or ever. As we approached the falls I had to admit it was one of the better looking little trout pools I had come across in quite awhile. The glide in by canoe was as silent as the 3 horse would permit. The air fragrant with spruce, the serenity jostled only once when we startled a momma moose and her calf lunching and munching in the short grass at the edge of the stream.

Little Boy Falls, cascading vertically a total of about five feet spilled into a wide pool just a short distance from the head of the Parmachenee. This looked for every bit virgin territory, quiet, private in every way holding the promise of brook trout of unfathomable lengths and girths. We pulled the canoe up short of the pool and managed to unload our stuff without disturbing the water.

Fishing gear like hunting gear. This is especially true if you're talking wading and fly fishing. With fly fishing there's rod assembly; attaching the reel, stringing the line, tying on the leader tie on the fly. So, it was only a short fifteen minutes later that we were in position, just below the falls, ready to engage a couple of brookies in a little tail dancing.

My peripheral vision butt in. A man-made structure we hadn't noticed at first nestled between a couple of birch trees about fifteen feet up the bank to the right of the falls.

It was a picnic bench and next to it an oil drum, aka garbage can. The ten feet of cleared forest around had been freshly manicured.

Dragging myself out of the stream to investigate, I discovered a brass plaque embedded in a large stone next to the bench. It commemorated the visit of Dwight David Eisenhower, our country's beloved 34th, an avid fishing enthusiast, to this very spot for a little R&R.

It seems that Eisenhower also had a hankering for a private, remote brookie spot, and Little Boy Falls was just his ticket. The difference between Dwight and I; the locals, in preparation for his trout fishing excursion to the Rangeley Lakes region had the local fish and game folks, accompanied by an untold number of secret service agents all wearing black, stock the area silly with enough brook, rainbow and browns to satisfy any chief executive.

Just then a truck drove by. Turns out that with a key to the locked gate where we had parked and past which we could drive no further, non- Bosebuck visitors could "easily" get to this private, utterly secret, very remote brookie paradise in a pick-up truck.

That evening at dinner as we sat down to our surf, turf and other fancy stuff we immediately noted that Jack's plate had a brand spanking new hornberg carefully placed in it's squeaky clean center. Muffled laughter could be heard wafting from the kitchen toward the dining room.

Two days later, not willing to concede defeat, we decided to wrap up the weekend with a side trip on the way out and wet a line around noon on the Swift River.

Fishing from just below the dam at the Swift River's headwaters, we knew we would be putting life and limb at risk. The first fifty yards of the Swift were capable of eating a fly fisherman alive in an instant carrying them down to a watery repose. It seemed worthwhile anyway in the hopes of salvaging an otherwise virtually trout-less Bosebuck excursion. The only one I had hooked and landed was a nice rainbow at the dam at the head of the Upper Magalloway just as thunder and lightening came crashing in. Since it was one of the only hook ups of that morning I determined that fate needed to be tempted and rather than retreat to shore I waved my fly rod, now potentially behaving like a lightening rod, in open defiance of the rumbling storm.

Back at the Swift an hour later still trout-less, tails between legs, we packed it in and headed back to the truck. We were tired and black fly bitten but really none the worse for wear. Besides we knew we were about to break out the remaining two icy brews along with a couple of liverwurst and red onion sammies slathered with hot mustard that we'd packed for the trip home.

Comfy in the truck and getting ready to dig in we were interrupted by a guy in a uniform... one of Maine's finest; a game warden. He had quietly strolled up to the truck and was now leaning in, elbow resting on the driver's side window ledge.

"Any luck?"

"Not much we admitted, understating the outcome of our side trip.

"Let's see your licenses, boys."

Then with impeccable timing, fluffy white kitten pranced up to the front of the cab and perched on Jack's shoulder, whereupon the warden inquired...

"Do you always take your kitten fishing?"

THE PERILS OF WILLIE FROM PITTSBURGH
Unity, Maine – Wednesday, October 16, 1985

Another lousy finish!

At least we got a little side show action when catcher Rich Gedman hit for the cycle as we embarrassed Toronto 13-1 at Fenway Park.

Speaking of warden's, one year Willie made the trip out from Pittsburgh by car for that fall's opening of the woodcock season, preferring to bring guns and gear neatly packed in the trunk of his car rather than hassle with checking his 20 gauge and shells through baggage at the airport.

And once again the scene of the crime would be Unity, but sadly a motel, as Henry's place where we logged for ten or twelve seasons in a row, was ashes.

The forecast was good, not so much the weather which almost always seemed to cooperate but our predictions of full larders and funny times. We were hardly ever disappointed.

About three days into the trip we piled into Willie's Blazer for the two or three mile ride to "the orchard". The orchard was one of the first and most dependable spots we frequented. On the high side of the road were a collection of ancient apples trees at varying distances from the road. On the low side was a massive alder run about the length of a football field and nearly as wide, terminating in a marsh. Invariably, we would push several to many partridge out of hiding in the apples, less often woodcock from the alders. Most escaped with their plumage intact to taunt us another day.

The road into this particular woodcock wonderland was a dead-ender with deep ruts and several areas where little streams spilled over its surface completely immersing its rock hard gravel base in six inches or so of water. This was not an easy access.

Given the difficult access and relative remoteness of this cover it came as a real surprise that after hunting for about an hour we found a representative of the Maine Department of Inland Fisheries and Wildlife standing by the Blazer as we trekked back to wrap up the afternoon.

"You guys doing a little bird shooting?" he inquired.

"No", I thought. What is it about a couple of guys carrying shotguns walking out of the wood, surrounded by dogs adorned with bright orange collars, bells ringing that would make you think we were doing a little bird shooting?

I said "Yup."

"Whose Blazer?" the warden wanted to know. Willie confessed that in fact it was his.

"Where you from?" he pressed.

"Pittsburg"

The warden took an abrupt step back from the Blazer, and although there is to this day some disagreement among us as to exactly what happened next, I contend that he slowly put a hand on his service revolver as he continued in a low and measured tone...

"If you're from Pittsburg how come you have Pennsylvania plates?"

ALL ROADS LEAD TO THE TIMBERDOODLE INN
Limerick, Maine – Wednesday, October 9, 1985

Is it "next year" yet?

The Timberdoodle Inn was a rambling old antique farmhouse in Limerick, Maine which just happened to be smack dab in the middle of some truly spectacular woodcock and grouse country.

The "Inn" was not open to the public, it being the private abode of Ernie, friend, fellow traveler in bird shooting and self proclaimed but really only marginal bon vivant.

The original house was constructed in the early 18th century making the first eight room, central chimney structure one of the earliest buildings in Limerick.

Like many early homes, his was railroad style with addition constructed over the course of nearly 125 years. The additions were connected by lumber if not by architecture. The Inn had two distinct additions, one added around 1820 and the other at the end of that century. There was, of course the obligatory attached barn to complete the picture.

Jack and I made occasional trips to Timberdoodle Inn for a visit with Ernie and his bird covers but none more memorable than the evening when we determined we were lost, sort of.

The prelude to this event was, of course, the traditional brew of black coffee and bourbon which seemed to always be our constant and steady companion for these sojourns north. It was a clear, crisp early October evening with everything lit up pretty nicely by a harvest moon.

Then about an hour into the hour and a half trip we made a wrong turn.

Seems we were having a little trouble distinguishing between the first and second fork in the road. We found ourselves driving in a the shadowy half light that was all the oak lined rural country road would permit. It took a drive of about a mile or two or possibly even three along that road until we finally concluded that we must have made a wrong turn. The occasional house or barn or fence that we could see were clearly, or more accurately unclearly not familiar to either one of us.

Being the quick studies that we were, we turned back. As we retraced our steps we began to have second thoughts, deciding then that the road was after all familiar and we just hadn't gone far enough to come upon some landmarks that we would surely recognize as familiar.

Of course the familiarity of the road that we were then experiencing was nothing more than the fact that we'd just come down the road several minutes before... no wonder it looked familiar.

Thereupon, we would turn around and head back remarking that "yes" the road was familiar. Gee, I wonder why the road (which we had just driving down moments before from the other direction) was now familiar.

Eventually we would reach and drive beyond the spot where we had last lost confidence in our decision and once more we began to feel that somehow, it was after all, not a road we had travelled before and that, yes, we were in fact on the wrong road after all.

It's embarrassing to admit just how many times we turned around and backtracked over our most recent backtrack.

This of course is either the definition of insanity or infinity… not really sure which.

Fortunately, I had had the foresight to stash a small, surprise cheese pizza under the seat and a brand new Buddy Holly tape had been locked, loaded and was blasting Peggy Sue thereby rendering irrelevant any concerns about our aimless wanderings. Until the pizza ran out it didn't seem to matter how many times we drove back and forth in the soothing isolation of that crisp near Limerick evening.

BORDER CROSSINGS AND OTHER FROZEN TURKEY MYTHS
Baie Comeau, Quebec Provence, Canada – June 1986

After a hiatus of eleven years we were back at the party. The 1986 Series against the Mets gave new meaning to the "Curse of the Bambino".

We were one I repeat one out away from winning the big enchilada. We led the Mets three games to two in the series. We held a two run lead when NY took their turn at the plate in the bottom of the tenth.

As easy as breaking sticks the first two Mets flied out.

The Nation cautiously prepared for jubilation, champagne glasses at the ready.

Then something hit the fan and the fans. Schiraldi gave up a hit to soon to be arch nemeses Gary Carter followed by another at the bat of Kevin Mitchell (who?). The hits were coming fast and furious with Ray Knight singling to score Carter and move Mitchell to third.

McNamara went to the bullpen for Stanley who promptly delivered a wild pitch. Mitchell trotted in to tie the game while Knight took second.

Then...

Mookie Wilson then hit a slow roller to Bill Buckner.

The good news... solace can be found in alder runs where you are unlikely to ever run into Bill Buckner.

Our group, went for a big time expedition in 86' when we booked a fly-in to remote Lac Aguenier, a part of the Manicouagan watershed in the province of Quebec. Based on the recommendations of a friend we would be making this dream trip to a remote lake in far be-gone Canada in pursuit of the fabled Big Brookies of the frozen north.

As it turned out, the lake contained only brook trout...but in breathtaking numbers. Both the fish and the numbers were big. These were not the little brookies of my youth nor of my days in Ossipee. These would turn out to be monster (or at least semi-monster) fish, sparkling and tantalizingly dark with shiny black backs, golden underbellies adorned with the usual brilliant little spots of red and yellow.

The plan was to travel by car up through Jackman, Maine and the Moose River Region to the border; cross, make a right then on along the north shore of the St. Lawrence. It would then be a quick 100 plus miles to our jumping off point in Baie Como. We were told that we would know when we reached Baie Como since that was where the road stopped. We would leave the cars there and slip into a vintage De Havilland Sea Otter for the flight to the lake.

When actually confronted with boarding a near antique Sea Otter, though tried and true as they may be, our group agreed that if necessary we should be ready to assist the plane by collectively flapping our arms should it be necessary in order to get air born.

The flight from Baie Como to Lac Aguenier takes about an hour and was accomplished at an altitude just slightly higher than the surrounding tree tops for most of the flight. In fairness, if you're a 40 plus year old plane packed with 7 adult males with pudgy edges who brought along pudgy gear, more gear and then even a little more gear, not to mention a peck of beer and bourbon you, too, would be lucky to skim just above the pines.

We split into two groups for the drive up. Jack, Hank and yours truly took the Mad Hatter's new Jeep and headed north. Eventually this would become known as Kamikaze One. The route that took us up through Jackman was on one of the states finest two laners.

It wasn't until we were approaching the border checkpoint that Mad informed us that he'd come up with a foolproof way to smuggle, yes, *smuggle* a little recreational contraband in with which we would be able to wile away the hours giggling and casting flies to rising brookies. I'll leave it to your imagination as to the specifics of the contra-b but suffice to say it would not be an uncommon addition to one's favorite brownie mix. Speaking of brownies, Hank had a suspicious looking cookie tin next to him on the seat.

His plan involved the purchase of a twenty-five pound turkey which would serve the dual purpose of becoming a staple of our diet for several of the six days we spent in our rural retreat as well as being a conveyer of "stuff".

After bringing said bird home from the market Hank pulled out the gizzard bag and inserted a couple of ounces of oregano look a like in a Glad bag. He then packed it back in with the gizzards. Whereupon, he froze the bird rock solid and packed it carefully into its own cooler for the trip north. Customs inspectors, he reasoned weren't paid enough to bother defrosting and rummaging through turkey innards for contraband.

What he failed to recognize was that his innate contempt for authority of any kind coupled with a lack of the most rudimentary skill set when it came to understanding the most ordinary questions, would put us in peril.

With Hank at the wheel we approached the border and coasted up to the waiting customs inspector. Hank rolled down his window. Jack and I sat with heads bowed in nervous prayer accompanied by sweaty palms and brows, silent at his side.

"Where you headed?" the inspector asked.

"Baie Como to go fishing", Hank.

"You have any guns?" the border constable inquired.

Now there was a curve ball Hank didn't expect. I would have thought the more likely questions at the border would be "Hiding any porn, any nearly extinct exotic mammals, been exposed to the plague, do you like hockey?" But nooooooo…. Any guns?

Hank owned a bunch of guns, a description of which he immediately began to rattle off to Mr. Inspector. "Yeah, I've got a 20 gauge double, a 12, my duck gun, a 30 06 for deer and a couple of pistols, a 45 and a 38. Oh, and a black powder…"

Trouble was it turned out the custom inspector meant WITH YOU! NOT AT HOME!

Having raised his suspicions to what were clearly dizzying heights even for a border agent we were summarily diverted to the Inspection Station for further examination. The Inspection Station being a menacing corrugated steel structure some seventy-five feet or so long and about two cars deep with no windows and six overhead doors, one of which was gently rising and beckoning to us as we slowly, reluctantly, in panic drove in the direction of the building.

My immediate fear, of course was that upon pulling inside we would see a ban saw in the corner surround by a half dozen defrosting turkeys that had been cut in half.

Once inside yet another officer of the border came in, turned, locked the door and proceeded with mirror on telescoping pole to go over every inch of our vehicle top, bottom and underbelly. He found waders, fly rods, vests, clothing, a first aid kit packed by the good doctor containing morphine which the inspector didn't seem to care about, various and assorted flies, a couple of decks of Bicycle cards and a frozen turkey which didn't garner even a second look.

HOME FREE!

It is customary at the border when the inspectors tear your stuff apart for them to wag a finger at the devastation indicating that it was then your job to put it all back together. This time I didn't feel put out as the three of us repacked the Jeep in record time, jumped in and began to back out as the overhead slowly rose behind us.

Hank couldn't resist, however a final goodbye and stopped just long enough to hold the cookie tin, top removed, out the window to offer the nice man one of our brownies.

Thankfully he declined.

So on we headed toward the land of endless brookies and our rendezvous with the Sea Otter.

All went well except for the following:

First, Hank, determined to make up the time lost at the border check began consistently driving at speeds in excess of 75 mph along a two lane highway through rural Quebec Provence. …yes, we got stopped.

Unfortunately, we got stopped just as we had fired up a couple of recreational… you know… and consequently found ourselves rolling the windows down at break-neck speed (for aeration purposes) as the Mountie gave chase and pulled us over. The fine was 150 dollars Canadian which Hank tried to negotiate on the spot. Jack and I were hastily digging through our wallets and tossing ten dollar bills in Hanks lap in an effort to steer the officer away from an on the spot cuffing.

Next, it rained. Not just a little. A lot. Thereby delaying our take off for Lac Aguenier by a day. But not being a crew content to sit back on our heels, we instead sat back on our butts, played poker from 10am 'til 6pm and polished off an inappropriate amount of brown stuff. By then we poured two of our group back into the Jeep and headed back for another overnight at the motel to wait for a morning takeoff.

We woke up to clear and sunny skies and a resulting smooth ride in to camp.

Once there, once unpacked, once in the boats and fishing we managed to catch so many brookies that first afternoon that the first conundrum popped up. What do you do with thirty or so fish and no refrigeration? Ice was at a premium, alternative and obvious uses were the priority, so packing in it for the trip home would be out of the question. It was than that we got to witness another Hank MacGyver-like creative miracle.

Faced with this challenge, Hank went to work and within a few minutes had rummaged through the little dump in the woods behind our cabin emerging with a somewhat beat up 3 foot length of discarded stove pipe and an old camp refrigerator, racks and all.

Presto... a smoke house was born. Not only did it work, it worked exceptionally well providing each of us with a cache of smoked trout to bring home to families as proof of our outdoorsman prowess.

HOODIE, ANNA, WATERCLOSETS & BLUEBERRY PIE
Dodge Pond, Lisbon, New Hampshire – October 17, 1987

Ah, back to a spot where we're comfortable. Fifth place

I met Anna in the first spring following Hoodies' death.

I'm not sure anyone in town remembered or for that matter ever knew what Anna Hood's husband's first name really was since nobody had called him anything but Hoodie since he was a kid, and that was over eighty years ago.

Hoodie was a local legend in the way many crusty farmers in rural New Hampshire are local legends. Everyone knew he was tough as a nail, resilient, skin dried to a leathery finish, overalls broken in real good. Hoodie had a homespun story to suit every occasion, more stories than it seemed possible one man could accumulate or make up in a lifetime. At least that's what I was told about him.

The widow Anna now lived alone on Dodge Pond a smallish puddle of water in Lisbon, New Hampshire. Her home just down from Ernie's mothers' cabin in a plain two story turn-of-the-century with attached barn. The house sat less than 10 feet from the edge of the pond, a modern day zoning nightmare. But both the home and Anna showed their age, the former sporting the faded remnants of what may have been its original and possibly only paint job, the latter looking over her shoulder at an eightieth birthday quickly receding from her memory.

We'd planned a two day fishing trip for whatever the Pond might produce, likely a bunch of small mouth and the occasional feisty little pickerel. Since it was my first trip to the cabin, Ernie had also planned a weekend that would include showing me around a few of his favorite fall woodcock and pa'trige covers.

On arriving, Ernie noticed that Anna was out front of her place stacking a little firewood, so we wandered down for introductions.

At fifty yards Anna appeared to be little more than a frail, thin, a somewhat diminished country lady. At three yards a revised description would be more to resemble that of her very recently demised husband; tough as a nail, resilient, skin dried to a leathery finish, hair thin enough to be a distant memory, her overalls broken in real good.

The house was even more rugged up close. Every window cried out for glazing, one of every three panes were cracked, the front steps just a touch tilted left to right.
"Morning, Anna", said Ernie. "What you bin up to?"

Whenever Ernie was talking to someone up country he seemed to have an aversion to the word "have". I guess it was just his way of adopting some sort of backcountry dialect.

"Blue berries". Anna was a woman of few words. "You?

"We're going to hit the pond for a little fishing, then poke around some of my old bird covers. See if we can spot a pa'tridge or two."

"Well," she replied "if you make it back early enough come down for a little pie and you can take a look at my new water closet. Picked blueberries fresh this morning", she said. My interest peaked. You don't often hear both the word pie and water closet in the same sentence. Turns out Anna had just had indoor plumbing installed for the first time and was clearly tickled pink over the thought of showing it off.

She and Hoodie had spent the better part of five decades in the old farmhouse never considering an upgrade from the original outhouse. Technically, I guess it was an in-house since it was located in a corner of the barn, accessible through the kitchen door a concession to the brutally cold January wind that had a habit of whipping across the pond and pounding on the back wall of the house. Nevertheless, she was proud of this latest home improvement and wanted to share it and a little blueberry pie with the neighbors.

It was a date!

At the end of that long and pleasant day that was filled with a few little bass and a peek at a bunch of interesting alder stands, we made it back to the cabin. After throwing a little water in my face and a little bourbon and water on my tonsils we wandered on down for dessert and a show at Anna's place.

Anna ushered us in through the barn door which then led to the side door which then brought us into a remarkably plain kitchen, beyond which we walked through a remarkably plain living room arriving finally into a remarkably plain dining room where we were seated at a remarkably plain oak table.

Furnishings were sparse, bordering on none. The wallpaper was a gray design which may have been a floral pattern at some point in time and set on a drab gray background; but I am not sure.

The pie, object of our visit, was doing it's blueberry best smelling thing having just come out of the oven. It sat prominently and proudly in the center of the table.

She had also made us a pot of coffee and motioned to each of our cups, offering to pour.

The pie was just as special as advertised and the coffee strong and hot enough to both cauterize the roof of your mouth and make both pie and java travel through your system like green corn through the new maid. That urge then, of course, reminded me of the other purpose of our visit.

"So, Anna, you said you have a new water closet," I said, thinking I might like to be among the first outsiders to use the new insider.

"Where is it?"

I'm not sure why I didn't notice the new water closet when we came into the dining room but there it was in plain sight in a corner of the room, completely plumbed in and ready to go. The logic of getting the toilet installed before putting up the walls to carve out a bathroom in a corner of the dining room escaped me. So what if the toilet lacked the necessary walls and door which would officially transform it into a more conventional and modest bathroom, so what?

Needless to say I waited until we returned to the cabin to address that pressingly urgent need.

DOING THE MAGALLOWAY TWO STEP
On Route 16 at the Magalloway near Wilson Mills, Maine – June 24, 1995

Obviously a strike shortened season is the key to victory. 86 wins and a first place finish in the AL East

But what's up with that trade for Pirate knuckleballer Timmy Wakefield? Jeez… How long can that last?

Jack and I pulled into the "Park & Fish" parking area just below the Magalloway dam on the Wilson Mills Road at around 8 am on the Friday of another Rangeley region extravaganza.

To our surprise there were no other cars, thus no competition for spots on that stretch of the river. Even after we'd spent the obligatory twenty minutes rigging up and squeezing into waders and wading boots we were still questioning why it was that no other fishermen were around. So strange it was beginning to take on a Twilight Zone quality.

But with the full landscape of spots along the river completely available we put our concerns aside and began the rugged little stream-side walk in search of a few trout and landlocked salmon.

As we went in I wondered aloud to Jack, "Are you sure the season is still open?" it being remarkable that we were still alone on the river.

"Yeah", Jack said definitively... "Pretty sure", he added.

About 50 yards along Jack decided to christen the day at an irresistible pool below a large rock that just seemed to have his name on it. The rock provided a quick little rife followed by a quick little run of cold Maine water, an ideally suited shelter for one of our scaly friends. I paused to watch as he propped himself against a boulder at the edge of this not so wade-able portion of the river. A single roll cast later he was on! A minute later Jack had landed a chunky, bright specimen of the landlocked salmon of beautiful silver persuasion, perhaps sixteen inches or so in length. A gem.

But there was something positively eerie about the luck that had descended on us that morning. Are you absolutely sure the season is still open?" he said.

"I can't believe we have the whole river to ourselves?"

"Don't you have a copy of the regs?" I said. "Usually, you get a copy when you buy a license."

"They're at home. Left them on the kitchen counter."

We followed the river down to the next irresistible and ominously vacant spot. This time I was in the water first and within a couple of minutes had a hit, managing to keep a reasonably sized fish on for a quick count of ten or so seconds before it liberated itself.

"I've got a feeling the season closed on the first... not the fifteenth". I said, it being the ninth day of the month as we continued nervously to discuss unspoken possibility that we were law breakers.

Shortly, it became apparent that we would not be able to enjoy the fact that we were alone any longer so we decided to abandon the stream and a take a short ride up the Wilson Mills Road to a little variety store three or four miles west across the New Hampshire line where Maine and New Hampshire licenses were sold. They would have a copy of the regs.

Well, it turned out that they had lots of things; rubber worms, day-glow orange knit caps, gummy bears and screw top Merlot but no fishing regulations.
Off we go!

After all the effort we expended hauling ourselves back to the car, shedding waders, and driving to ye Olde Backwater Emporium & Bait Shoppe did not resolve our question about the season dates. What did resolve the issue as to whether the season was open or not was that upon our return to the parking area we found it in dire need of an attendant given all the cars that had shown up while we were gone. This taught us something about ourselves that for the sake of my grandchildren I hope and pray is not genetically linked.

We have always assumed that if things are going well, something must be wrong.

For when it comes to fishing were it not for bad luck it seems at times we'd have no luck at all.

BETCHA CAN'T SAY
"COBBOSSEECONTEE" 3 TIMES FAST
Lake Cobbosseecontee - Augusta, Maine – Saturday, August 10, 1996

Considering that we started the season with 6 wins and 19 losses,
I guess a third place finish wasn't so bad.

The well known expression "Never let a cheap wine breathe" was born on one of our epic bass fishing excursions to Cobbosseecontee Lake near Augusta. This same trip also gave rise to the now familiar corollary expression, "Never let a cheap bastard buy the wine!" Father Cabrera Red Table Wine was the only wine in over twenty years of these trips to survive, sipped once, the remainder then studiously un-drunk, making the round trip home.

Of more interest on this particular trip, however, was the saga of the lost sailors or "Where are those idiots, it's getting dark" and the near tragic, "I'm pretty sure he left his eyebrows in the kitchen".

First, the lost sailors. Sailing? No, except for the metaphor not so cleverly hidden in "Yo, ho, ho and a bottle of rum" which for us was more likely to be Yo, ho ho and a bottle of Jim Beam bourbon not rum. Some say I was born a couple of bourbons short of a full load. I've recently cut back though. Each night I now only drink about a fifth of my favorite bourbon.

We, Ben and I, were wrapping up a nifty afternoon plugging for small mouth bass in a few of the placid little coves near our cabin. Our mode of travel was a fourteen foot aluminum craft just perfect for bobbing around aimlessly on that warm August afternoon.

We were finishing up the day just around a bend which would be a straight shot across the lake back to our cabin as dusk began to settle in... we thought. A bend from which we should have been able to see within a distance of a hundred yards or less, not only the cabin, but its' dock and a few friends already well invested into the cocktail hour.

We soon learned that there are bends and then there are bends. Suffice it to say we got a little confused, once again. Rounding said bend it came as a bit of a surprise that no dock, no friends and no cabin were anywhere to be seen. In fact no civilized shoreline was in sight just more coves, inlets, islands and dreaded bends. We spent the next hour circling, circling again then circling some more in search of anything that looked familiar. It turned out that the most familiar thing would be the dark which we had no trouble seeing since it appeared to be everywhere.

Eventually, dumb luck led us back to the cabin but not before leaving a trail of propeller scarred rocks and a chunk of the boat's propeller in our wake. These were rocks that lurked just below the water's surface and were clearly marked as hazards... just not clearly marked in a day-glow paint that might have been a little more helpful given our circumstance.

This grueling day was thankfully followed by good cheer, good spirits, good grub and a little poker... which leads us to the eyebrow incident. The card table sat six but only five wanted to play that evening. Ron was a little more interested in dinner than cards and so had been investing his free time in the kitchen immersed in the early stages of rustling up some grub. Problem was he had no idea how to turn on the oven in the gas stove.

The disappearance of his eyebrows in this circumstance is invariably preceded by a pronounced "WHUMP," signifying that an accumulated cloud of gas has decided to ignite and do its singy thing.

Looking at the glass as half full, in addition to removing eyebrows the mini gas explosion provided the unexpected benefit of giving one, Ron, the appearance of recently having been lashed down under a sunlamp with a sunburn.

I know you'll find it hard to believe but it's true; Ron failed to see the humor in this.

KOKADJO AND "POPS" CAMP
Kokadjo, Maine at Moosehead and the Roach River – Spring 1997

Rookie Nomar Garciaparra made the Fenway scene this year achieving almost immediate superstar status. As Rookie of the Year he hit .306 with 30 homers and 98 RBIs.

Jimy Williams' in his first season as manager led the charge to a disappointing fourth.

There was a spell of five or six seasons when our latest hot spot had become the Roach River, which fed the north end of Moosehead Lake. It's not advisable to plan on holding your breath while getting there since it pretty much takes forever. Up the Maine pike, then a series of relatively uninteresting back roads on the way to the town of Moosehead.

The final leg is up along the east shore road which will take you to Kokadjo Sporting Camps, where our host Fred Candeloro, a Revere, Mass. lad who took a hankering to the great outdoors and ski mobiles in particular.

148

He and wife Marie had given up the city life to become the most noteworthy entrepreneurs in the town of Kokadjo. Correction the only entrepreneurs in Kokadjo.

We always requested the same accommodations, "Pop's" Camp which was an extremely interesting log cabin with a decidedly right leaning propensity, much like a couple of the fellows I travelled with. The cabin was leaning at perhaps 15 degrees out of true vertical, so much so that the outside wall had been propped up to protect against a tip over. Three or four telephone poles had been driven securely into the earth and wedged against the building.

Normally, we tried to time our trip to arrive on a Thursday around 4pm or so in time to give ourselves a couple of approaching twilight hours on the river before settling in for the evening.

The last time we went up, Jack and I were taking the obligatory and necessary fifteen to twenty minutes getting our gear pulled together. You know, assemble the rod, tie on the leader, select and tie on the first fly, pull on the waders and finally, wincing force the wad of oversized wader bootie into a slightly undersized boot.

We were going to stroll down to the Dump Pool. Yeah, there really is a Dump Pool so named for the remnants of broken bottles, tin cans and other bits of garbage that greet you at waters edge. Once past that first impression, however, the stream was pretty nifty. A deep run in the far bank at the first swing in the river below the pool invariable held a land lock or two along with a few scrappy brook trout.

We had just finished suiting up when I noticed a familiar buzz circling my ear. A quick pat of my vest pockets produced no object the size or shape of mosquito repellant. "Hey, Jack, you got any bug juice?"

Piercing the sweaty, muggy Kakadjo spring air came his dreaded but inevitable reply… "No".

It was at this point that I came to believe in miracles. Unwilling to turn back with evening approaching we steeled ourselves for what we were certain would be several hours of casting for trout punctuated by constant bug slapping. Jack was less concerned than I since I, you may recall had the notorious history of being singled out in any group of fishermen as prime meat and the prime target for our buzzy little friends. No amount of repellant ever seemed to be enough, no matter how thoroughly I drenched a kerchief and wrapped it around my neck the little beasts pursued me relentlessly.

So it was to my amazement that right there at the Dump Pool in Kokadjo I discovered a odd truth. All my previous attempts to shield myself from attack by slathering myself with repellant, repellant which then combined with the sweat from summer heat, must have caused some chemical reaction that had the reverse effect than intended. There, naked of repellant, I got not a single mosquito bite.

Hallelujah!

I've since disposed of my rather imposing stockade of repellants, liquid, spray, stick, scented, unscented and otherwise.

RUNNING WITH THE BULLS
(...not to mention the Bobs)
Oquossoc, Maine – Tuesday, August 18, 1998

We were headed toward a number two finish behind Cleveland for the Division title but it was August and the brookies were thick in the Kennebago, no time for baseball.

There are some people for whom mastering the subtle art of the perfect fly cast comes as naturally as breathing. Some who intuitively understand and feel the rhythms and the nature of the union achieved between hand, wrist, rod and reel when softly laying down a #20 midge twenty feet out into the still waters of a remote beaver pond.

Then there was my brother, Bob.

When I watched Bob cast it was anything but as natural as breathing, it actually made you hold your breath.

But then what else would you expect from a wrestling coach, former linebacker and high school track and field star, the finesse normally associated with a tap dancer?

Bob was undeterred by the fly fishing awkwardness his brawn created and always seemed determined to learn the fine art of the cast anyway. I, as the older, oft imitated, somewhat unjustifiably admired big brother had been given the assignment of being his lifelong fly fishing coach.

My coaching days really began with Bob from the get-go. He dogged my tracks religiously from the age of three or four, cane pole in hand as I wandered down to the mighty Rockaway River for afternoon encounters with a few unsuspecting perch, sunnies and bluegills. He was forever leaning over my shoulder observing my night crawler extracting technique after a spring storm coaxed them to the surface.

His room was a-clutter with jars of salamanders, a box with a box turtle and the previous evening catch of now deceased fire flies.

However, despite his love of the outdoors and his tenacious copying of every move, every interest of his older brother the finer points of fly fishing seemed to elude him completely.

He was a brawny kid. His fly casting was more reminiscent of the way he threw a javelin or for that matter a sack of potatoes than the grace that activity demanded.

Frequently, the frenzied slashing motion of his aggressive back and forth windup to a cast produced a slew of froth and bubbles for yards in every direction surrounding his waders.

No matter. He was just as I was, content to be there. Together. And it never really mattered where "there" was.

Although, "there", frequently was the Kennebago River. It was the near perfect fly casting stream, shallow, crystal clear it's banks lined with alders, tall grass and the occasional stand of aspen. It's headwaters, Lake Kennebago, made headlines each May with the departure of ice and the simultaneous arrival of "sports" to woo the not so elusive landlocked salmon. This included such dignitaries as Herbert Hoover an avid fly fisherman and early arrival in the chilly North Country air of 1939.

We would hike in parallel to the stream along the gated access road. It was about a mile, seeming in waders to be much further, to the first bridge. We would then wade and fish our way out, usually a four or five hour stroll in the brookie infested waters.

Our fishin' hole of choice when we chose to avoid the long walk in was a busy, often crowded little spot near the end of the rivers run named the Steep Bank Pool. It was drive-right-up-to and wade-able and was only five minutes or so from our rental.

The last time we found ourselves fishing there was on an early outing on a particularly windy August morning. The day also featured clear skies and temps getting ready to run up later in the day to the mid 70's.

I was standing in the stream and had been rummaging through my stash of flies searching for the perfect buggy imitation to start the morning off. For the average fly fisherman this is a ritual filled with anticipation, optimism and the belief that the cosmos may finally be generous in return for their diligence. I never hurry when selecting a fly, thinking that somehow if I take just a little more time I'll get it right this time.

This particular morning, even though I knew it, the fly I selected had never so much as gotten a second look from any trout to whom I had previously presented it. I went with a bead-headed nymph. For the uninitiated among you it's a pattern meant to resemble the larval stage in an insects' life. In this case the fly had been weighted with a little copper colored BB to give it the sinking power it would need to get down in full view of my prey.

I learned that day that weighted flies handle a little differently on a windy day than their almost weightless cousins. That little BB head tended to make my line behave

153

more like a sling shot than a fly rod, propelling the fly at
death defying speed through the air.

That morning when BB met wind I ended up with a
particularly dangerous combination, resulting with the fly,
during its return flight in preparation for my final forward
cast, was pushed just enough by the breeze to my left to
lodge firmly in my cheek.

I was unable to muster the courage to rip the little #10 sucker
out since the rear view mirror of the car didn't give me the
kind of look at it that would make me feel comfortable when
performing this minor surgery. Neither was I comfortable
with my brother's offer of assistance. It seemed to me that
he might have trouble steadying his hand at the same time he
struggled to muffle his laughter.

So off we went back to the rental where with the help of a
couple of morning bourbons and a razor I made the
extraction.

Now, one would think that perhaps this experience would
cause me to be leery of yet a second trip to the Kennebago
that day.

Not so.

This was to have been our annual trudge in and wade out
day.

Typically, we would begin with an hour or so at Steep Bank
then hop out and walk to the bridge. This produced some
very predictably relaxing downstream wading, as well as
usually producing a batch of brook trout in the six to twelve

inch range all of which we would return to be fished another day.

So back we went and passing this time on the Steep Bank we got right to the business of hiking into the bridge.

The first couple of hours went along as planned. Here a brookie, there a brookie, everywhere a brookie-brookie. Even Bob was unable to deter their ravenous appetites although whip the water into a frothy brew he did.

Then that Pamplona-Kennebagoian thing happened. Not to take anything away from my fellow bull running compatriots in Spain, but I'm pretty sure they never had to make their mad dash in front of the bulls decked out in fishing waders and sporting a fully loaded vest while carrying a fly rod.

Here's the deal. We were about mid-thigh deep in water as we approached a big bend about half way back to the car when we heard a grunt.

"Grunt?" I queried. Bob shrugged and looked at me, the all-knowing big brother for an answer.

"It came from just around the bend", I said belaboring the obvious as we continued to cautiously work our way downstream.

Upon rounding the bend we were met by Miss Moose and Mr. Bull Moose having lunch in what I'm sure they thought was their very own private backwater alcove of the stream where moose lunch stuff was growing in abundance just below the surface.

No, Mr. Bull was not of the well-known bulls of Pamploma, Spain, pointy horns and all. Still, a thousand plus pounds or so of irritated moose was a pretty close second.

He looked upset and prepared at the drop of a hat to do a tap dance on one or both of us. I'm not sure quite how to describe his expression but he stopped eating, stared directly at us and snorted. Then he took a step toward us. I personally preferred the snorting to the stepping

Instinctively we began to edge our way back up stream.

"Bob", I said, "move very, very slowly. Don't provoke him. Let's see if we can get up the bank and onto dry land just in case he charges".

"Are you crazy? You can't outrun a charging moose."

I'd waited a lifetime for that straight line.

"I don't have to out run the moose, Bob. I just have to out run you." (Would someone with a snare drum out there please give me a rim shot?)

We managed to back our way slowly upstream and around the little bend without provoking a charge by the bull, but now faced a new dilemma. The only practical way back to the car was downstream. Going downstream would mean wading past the lunching moose and running the risks associated with that boneheaded approach or climbing out of the river and walking fifty yards or so on dry land before getting back in.

Sounds like a simple enough choice until you realize that the phrase "simpler said than done" was clearly made for this situation. The far bank of the stream was immediately met by a hillside with a grade steep enough to prevent us from walking down that side. It was also the bank closest to and most likely to be the path of retreat of the moose.

The near bank was a tangle of alders and muck so thick you could throw your hat at the ground and it might not hit for three days. The brush appeared to be a kissing cousin of quicksand. Considering the size of the moose the quicksand option didn't seem so bad.

The fifty yards translated into about thirty minutes of slow, sweaty trudging. Remember it was August and we were both sporting rubber pants.
Did I mention the mosquitoes?

Despite catching around thirty or forty brookies that day it would forever be known for the lunch we shared with the moose.

PULASKI AIN'T NO PLACE FOR OLD MEN OR OLD VOLVOS

The Salmon River - Pulaski, New York – April 7, 2002

The Sox finished in second place. Ho, hum.
In the spring of 99' Jack and I decided to take a break from the now redundant trip to the Pere Marquette in Western Michigan for steelhead to see if a spot a little closer to home could yield similar results.

The trip to the PM was over 900 miles and ate up two eight hour days of driving. Bummer! Pulaski and the renowned Salmon River were a mere 360 miles and if hard pressed you could hold you breath for the 6 or so hours it took to get there.

The Salmon River is one of the many feeder streams to the great lakes that have benefited from the importation of steelhead in 1885 from the McCloud River in California, then subsequently propagated at the Caledonia Hatchery in New York. By 1900 self-propagating numbers of steelhead were well established throughout the great lakes.

The River is a little larger than I'm either used to or comfortable with. On average it runs about fifty yards or more in width, seems to have a consistently strong current and features a slippery bottom, just the ticket for then 58 year old knees.

The other tricky part about the Salmon River however is, although the river has an abundance of fish it is also regulated for flood control by a dam. This makes predicting the fish-ability of the river a potential problem since a little excess spring rain can easily turn the waters into a torrent of angry, muddy, upper New York run-off depending on the

158

flow rate the local gate keeper deems appropriate. He deemed it appropriate to open the flood gates for our weekend sojourn.

Sometimes the bear eats you.

In 2002 we returned to the Salmon and hunkered down for the three day fishing extravaganza having made the trip in my very used 740 Volvo sedan, as it was my turn to drive.

No biggie. We shot out to mid NY and our Pulaski accommodations in about five plus hours, enjoying scenic western Massachusetts and the lovely NY Thruway along the way.

The place we stayed was pretty comfy, an old farmhouse with all the modern amenities; i.e. running water coming both in and going out, a modern kitchen and best of all direct access to the river.

We had even arranged for a guide for the first day having learned that maximizing our enjoyment and results on any of the new trips was really enhanced if we loosened up on the wallets and let someone show us the ropes.

The river was so high that actually wading in it would have been impossible. It was so muddy and swift that I was convinced that any fish still in the river could only be there if it had swallowed large rocks as ballast.

But our guide was a gamer. Even though he knew there wasn't a prayer we would hook up in a river as swollen as the Salmon was that day he cheerily spent all day changing our fly patterns, moving us from spot to special spot in the river, encouraging us with reports of recent successes that his clients had had. By the end of it we were zero for zero on fish. Our guide was a little embarrassed and we were staring at two more days of what we knew would be an identical experience... zero for zero.

It was, therefore two days later that along with a goodly dose of humility Jack and I packed up the Volvo and headed down old Route 11 toward home.

We got about two miles when the 740's engine cut out and we coasted to the side of the road.

The last car that was simply enough engineered to allow me to perform a fix a little two-seater manufactured in the UK by Peter Morgan. It was simple enough in design that one could rebuild the engine in a weekend using a screwdriver and duct tape. Then they went all computer-y on me.

So we stood there with the hood up staring into the tangle of wires, metal objects, pulleys and belts hoping for a miracle. None appeared until a nice young fellow with pretty fair mechanical knowledge stopped, took us under his wing and helped diagnosed the problem. Our alternator had decided to end it's useful life.

In the world of automobile repair this is not big deal, unless it's Sunday, you're in rural New York and you also happen to be driving a FOREIGN CAR.

What do you suppose the odds are of finding a mechanic who works on Volvos or for that matter a mechanic who has access to a replacement alternator for your foreign car?

Yeah, that's what I thought too. One in a million would be a good guess.

Alas it was not to be... so our new young friend suggested an alternator alternative. Buy a couple of new batteries that could be swapped out every hour or two and nurse the car home where it could be fixed.

This plan just might work.

So off we went to local Pep Boys for a couple of batteries, installed one and were back on the road within an hour or so, Pulaski in the rear view mirror!

The first battery change didn't become necessary until we were almost in sight of the Massachusetts state line. The warning sign of impending battery near death was the illumination of a little red light on the dash. So wrenches in hand we swapped the battery over in exchange for the other new one and we were on our way again. This time we made it to the Worcester area when it looked like another trade was in order.

Here of course is where we made a tactical error in thinking that buying a third battery rather than simply swapping the now somewhat refreshed first battery back into position would be the smarter approach.

Trouble was it was now late afternoon on Sunday and even in the thriving metropolis of Worchester we were having trouble finding a store that sold batteries.

After about a ½ hour plus of flitting back and forth between exits off 290 and the little strip malls we kept seeing we resigned ourselves to the probability that the two batteries we already had would have to do.

We had now wasted precious time that could have contributed to our progress home. Instead, we noticed that the shadows everywhere were growing distressingly longer as evening was gearing up for an appearance.

Now we were in a race against the clock. We swapped the battery again, crossed our fingers and got back on the Interstate trail.

Headlights normally are turned on when it gets dark. Dark hit around 45 minutes later when we were cruising up 495 on what was the last hour long leg of our trip. Here's the dilemma. If I turned the headlights on the battery would drain very quickly bringing us to a halt. If I drove in the dark some cement bridge abutment would likely bring us to a halt. I compromised. Without headlights turned on I began to follow a car that was travelling at a moderate speed in the slow lane just in front of me. I followed at a distance which allowed me to get a peek at the road ahead of that car without tailgating too closely.

Each time another car approached us from the rear I would give them a short blast of my headlights and more to the point tail lights just to let them know I was there.

They would then pass me, flashing their high beams to let me know that my lights were not on. We continued on our merry way sans lights.

This seemed to work fairly well for the better part of ten or so miles as I continued to trail the same car. It then began to dawn on me, however, that the driver of the car we had been following might be wondering why they were being stalked by a car with their headlights turned off who intermittently flashed those headlights into their rear view mirror.

As we zipped along occasionally passing under the overhead lights that were illuminating the exits I noticed that the driver was alone and a woman.

We were approaching an exit around Westford when the woman began to slow down and move toward the exit ramp. As luck would have it our little red light coincidentally made another appearance signaling the end to our alternator experiment so we too moved toward the exit.

It was only later that I realized that she must have interpreted our last move, to follow her off the exit as the final straw. So to the anonymous lady from Westford, MA... my apologies for any sleepless nights that may have ensued.

Regards... the Steelhead Stalkers

IT'S SLOW LEARNERS DAY AT THE PERE MARQUETTE
Wahalla, Michigan - October 19, 20, 21, 22, 2004

Our now annual run to the salmon run featured blue bird skies, no rain and the Sox in the playoffs again.

Listening to the 2004 American League Championship Series between the Red Sox and Yankees turned out to be the high point of our salmon run to the Pere Marquette.

The Sox won the series four games to three, after trailing three games to none.

Over four glorious fall days Boston exorcised its ghosts.

The 86 year drought was over, traded with the Yanks for their self imposed self destruction, the biggest postseason collapse of all time. (At least up to that time since the Sox still had the dreaded 2011 season to look forward to)

The radio reception was scratchy at best until we unleashed Eric the Engineer who summarily fixed the problem. (He adjusted the antenna, duh!)

We arrived at Duffy's Cabin at Barothy down three games to zip and only half-heartedly decided to tune in game four expecting the worst. At least, we thought, this impending sweep by New York would be offset by the fact that we were comfortably ensconced in a great little cabin on the bank of the PM with an adequate supply of liquid refreshments.

Mike Mussina had pitched game one, perfectly... for six innings. The Sox had brought it close but failed to seal the deal.

Olerod tipped the game the Yanks way with a homer in game two, setting the stage for a twenty-two hit lopsided win for New York in game three.

The Yankees were ahead by one run in the ninth in game four. We were settled in next to the fireplace in Duffy's resigned to the inevitable WHEN DAVE ROBERTS STOLE SECOND!!!!

On Wednesday the Sox become the first and only team in MLB history to win a series after being down three games to none and, yes the salmon were running.

When I think about the Pere Marquette I'm reminded that some things in life are experienced "better late than never".

We'd first been told about the river shortly after Willie had been exiled to a new job and new life in Pittsburgh, leaving the bucolic abandoned farms, dirt roads and small brookie streams of the east for the rest of us to continue plundering.

To his credit he would turn up every October for the annual trip to Henry's place and on the first occasion of his return after his move to Pittsburgh he informed us that Nirvana indeed existed in places other than New England. Willie had made the acquaintance of a fellow traveler in fly fishing who was a member of the Pere Marquette Club.

We, of course, up to that time, had never heard of it. So he proceeded to describe in great detail the previous fall run of steelhead and king salmon that he'd fished in this amazing river. He even brought pictures in which giant salmon and steelhead were carefully posed in trophy-like repose on the grassy banks of the river.

The Pere Marquette River is among the most heart stopping trout, salmon and steelhead infested rivers south of Alaska, particularly if you're into wading. It flows gently for the most part as it winds through Michigan's western flatlands seeking out the big water. As it moves inevitably toward Lake Michigan it runs through some of the most rural, poverty stricken and barren portions of the Wolverine state. Its' browns are legendary, its' hatches of mayflies, stoneflies and caddis, the stuff of fireside reading and ranting.

Being slow learners, however, we were not immediately moved to action even when presented with the photographic evidence of Willie's successes at this great, new fishing hole. It would be nearly fifteen years later when by chance my nephew Eric from Ann Arbor decided to take up fly fishing and equally by chance invited me to join him that fall at this great new place he'd discovered, the Pere Marquette River.

I finally made it to the banks of the PM for my first "steely" experience in '94 and proceeded to hook up on my very FIRST cast.

We had arranged for a guide for the trip down the river as I'd never fished for steelhead before

Eric (nephew), Joe (husband of niece) and I met Greg the Guide at the Pere Marquette River Lodge in the Orvis endorsed outfitters shop about 5 am. I'm quite sure fish don't get up that early but never mind. He inspected our gear; first, Eric's who passed muster with flying colors as did Joe's.

Then he came to me, observing that my brand new 9 foot 9 weight had neither a proper reel nor proper line, and by the way did I realize that the water was a little chilly for wearing ultra lights. You see I had reasoned in packing for the trip that we would be fishing out of a drift boat and only standing in an ankle deep stream for short periods of time. Turns out I should have invested right then and there in a new pair of waders since the PM in early April can be a chilly spot.

Ultra lights! My ultra lights had the insulating characteristics of talcum powder; ultra lights in which I would spend a very long eight hours in and out of a drift boat and on the Pere Marquette. Would have been just as well off wearing the bottoms to last years Halloween costume because it would certainly have been reasonable to accuse me of being a horse's ass for the equipment I'd chosen to bring.

Never mind the ultra lights. Our guide was still lobbying for me to invest in a new reel. I said "What does a decent reel go for?" (I would remind you we are in an Orvis store). He said I could get a serviceable one starting around about seventy-five bucks.

I said that where I came from I could get two reels for that kind of money with enough left over to buy lunch for a week.

Somewhat indignantly I threw in that seventy-five bucks sounded like what the store might be able to get next year for a reel if they got lucky and were also able to add 30 percent or so to the price due to inflation.

"Yeah", he replied. "You're right. That might be next year's price, but you have to remember even if you have to pay next year's price now you get to use the reel this year."

This bit of impeccable logic did not persuade me. I passed on the reel. I did however give in on the line at $30.

We proceeded next to the fly display case. Our guide explained that he would equip us with the deadliest steelhead flies known to man. We would be using what we needed to during the float and settle up upon our return. I'm thinking a half dozen flies each at $2.50 to $3.00 apiece.

"Yeah", he commented on seeing my disbelief at the number of flies he was bringing along.

"They're a little pricey, but they're so good you have to go behind a tree to tie them on. Otherwise the fish come out of the river to get them which gives us an unfair advantage."

Apparently, I was not thinking steelhead since he picked out well over 100 flies to sustain us during our float. He put them in a couple of plastic boxes which he then stuffed in his vest. Upon our return, a count of the days remaining flies revealed that he had only slightly overestimated our losses to the river.

We had left eighty nine flies impaled on sunken logs and wedged in the crevices of sneaky little rocks along the river bottom. Also, left behind were virtually all of the steelhead the river held who had managed to deftly avoid our clutches.

In retrospect it might have been more satisfying to have simply stood at the river's edge, tossed my Wheatley fly box into the current and shouted "All right, already! YOU WIN, YOU WIN!"

This proved to be a valuable lesson as it launched the fly tying phase of my stream side adventures. If I learned to tie my own flies just think of the savings. As soon as I made the necessary initial investment in a variety of fly tying vises, several rooster and hen capes, assorted rabbit fur, eagle and other feathers, elk hair, bobbins, threads and threaders, a bodkin, hair stacker, rotary whip finishser, special scissors and hackle pliers as well as a fly tying workbench in which to store the above I would be well along the way to big, big savings.

As an aside, the next year I brought my cache of freshly tied salmon and steelhead flies to christen them along the banks of the Pere Marquette. Let's just say that the appearance thereafter of newly posted signs in the areas I fished warning that "No Wake" should be made is a testament to my heavy-handed execution of the patterns.

Eventually, I mastered the art of tying salmon flies (at least based on some pretty nifty results) with the introduction a couple of years later to the river of my signature fly, the "Purple Death" salmon streamer.

Then in '95 I dragged Jack along for his first shot at the river. Our destination was Barothy Lodge on a lower portion of the river which provided accommodations a cut above what we were normally accustomed to. Barothy was a quick left hand turn out of Wahalla, then another left at Anne's Gift Shop on the road to nowhere. The good folks at Barothy feature a selection of fifteen cabins and a private shoreline for the exclusive use of their guests. We were put up that first year in the Rainbow Cabin with its' promise of a pot of steelhead gold should we find its' end.

And Jack did find the end of the Rainbow. By the end of his first year, we both ended up being firmly hooked on the virtues of the river. Multiple trips were planned over the next decade. We usually went in early April when there were frequently still small patches of snow in the woods.

Temps lingered in the mid-forties during the day and when combined with the chilly spring-fed waters of the Pere Marquette kept our teeth a-chattering.

That first year we lived the life of Riley in our palatial chateau of six bedrooms, replete with cathedral ceilings, fully equipped kitchen, a pool table in the basement and, oh goody, a hot tub room to which we made a habit of retiring after about every three or four frigid hours on the river.

The place was maybe fifty yards from what turned out to be one of the best stretches of water and spawning redds on the river. The first morning Jack planted himself in waist deep water just below a bend that quickly straightened out and flowed over a ten foot redd before plunging into a black hole of undetermined no-bottom-ness.

Turns out it was a black hole full of very aggressive steelheads parked just behind the rather large female who occupied the redd.

It was from these depths that Jack hooked up an impressive number of steelhead. If I told you he hooked fifteen it would be an under-estimation; twenty-five the proverbial fish tale.

What was however most memorable was that each time we retreated to the hot tub sanctuary some nephew or other, perhaps a brother- in- law would quickly settle into the same spot. Following Jack's lead they would toss the exact same pattern to the exact same spot in the river, allow the same drift and produce no results whatsoever.

I would like to report that the steely fishing has been this good every other time we've made it to the PM. I would like that but I am unable to do so since we've been skunked on several occasions.

Steelhead are a wary bunch and like most trout are smarter than the average fisherman. Consequently, our trips to the PM expanded to include the fall salmon run which is a whole heap easier while still holding out the promise of the occasional steelhead.

Some trips were so successful that the same redd and gravel run that produced such good results for Jack on his first trip more than just occasionally held fifteen or twenty salmon at a time.

One year I found myself sporting a broken left arm, which of course brought new meaning to the word "cast".

As luck would perversely have it, I seemed to hook up constantly and was beginning to wear out a little from the strain of tugging at these monsters with just my right arm.

It was then that Jack tells me that he heard me say, as I tossed a fancy, giant chartreuse streamer into the middle of a pod of king salmon. "Please don't let the big one take it!"

Some days you eat the bear and some days the bear eats you... one of my better bear eating days.

**casting about for king salmon
on the Pere Marquette**

THE LEGENDARY JAMES ERASTUS WOOD
... or how to eat like y'all from Tennessee
Nashville, Tennessee and Terra Ceia, Florida – at various formative moments during my youth

James Erastus had no time for baseball. Pity.

My uncle Jim was an imposing fellow, all five feet seven inches of him. He held dual citizenship both as a Tennessean as well as a Floridian of the old school from birth through death.

Truth be told Uncle Jim mostly had a soft spot in his heart and head for the family's ancestral home in Terra Ceia where our side of the Wood family and his would reunite occasionally. We would join him to vacation summers when Grandma Laura Tate was still kicking.

James Erastus
Terra Ceia, Florida 1942

When I was six or so, my first memory of my uncle was as the gruff, tough, unbending sole sibling to my mom. At sixty pounds and four feet two I was compelled by obvious physical realities to look up to the man.

This is the uncle who decided I should learn the fine art of barrel fishing. He would fill the bottom of a couple of big old oak barrels with rocks for ballast, get me in one while he got in another and away we'd paddle into Tampa Bay.

172

After baiting a rig with live mullets we would let them run until an unsuspecting tarpon would hook up one or the other of us and provide a ride around the bay before it was time to cut the line and return home.

This is the uncle who gave me my first pocket knife on my eighth Christmas along with a box full of Confederate musket balls, Confederate uniform buttons, real Indian arrowheads and about three hundred dollars in Confederate money.

This is the uncle who gave me my first and only instruction in the art of cast netting mullets in the shallows of Tampa Bay. He then showed me how to smoke them in his homemade smokehouse. Then he drew up plans so I could build my own.

This is the uncle who taught me the proper way to hold a live chicken while introducing it to Mr. Axe.

This is the uncle who took me surf casting off Bradenton Beach where we waded in, caught a few fish which he proceeded to string up, then tie the stringer to his belt. Then waist deep in the surf he felt the tug of a small shark trying to liberate his catch for lunch.

This is the uncle who instructed me in the fine art of squirrel hunting. Some men would say "Why squirrels?" I say "Why not!" This is a fair enough question for those among us with no roots in Tennessee or for those without access to a batch of yummy, traditional Tennessee squirrel recipes.

But to the deed at hand; hunting down and dispatching of squirrels, red, black grey or for that matter those of any other persuasion. The squirrel hunt was perhaps the easiest of all hunting activities to teach a ten year old armed with a pellet gun and boundless enthusiasm for the task.

If you've ever approached a squirrel a couple of things become readily apparent. First, they never get too far from a tree, usually a tall one, and they immediately position themselves out of your line of sight on the opposite side of the tree. They're not particularly concerned with scampering up the tree, just putting the tree between you and them.

If you decide to pursue this little game and begin to walk slowly around the tree you'll notice that they will scamper to the other side of the tree but only progress up the trunk slightly. What squirrels have apparently not figured out about this strategy is that the more you circle the tree forcing them to slowly climb higher and higher the thinner the trunk becomes until ultimately it's girth is no longer sufficient to hide them.

...years later this appeared in the local rag
UPLAND CULINARY DELIGHTS
West Newbury, Mass. – January 27, 2011

Dougherty praised for his creative game dishes...sadly not his fishing or shooting skills

Special to the *Upland Game Cooking Chronicles*
West Newbury, MA January, 27, 2011

As a kid and budding outdoorsman West Newbury local J.C. Dougherty learned to live by the house rules. That is, whenever he would wander up from the river near his childhood home with a stringer of catfish, trout or bass the ruler of the house and maker of the rules, mom insisted "You catch 'em, you clean 'em, you cook 'em"

With ancestral roots in Georgia, Tennessee and Florida most of the meals Dougherty patched together as an adolescent included the predicable sides of hush puppies, grits and corn bread.

One quirk about his cooking has been, he points out that he does not like to follow recipes. "I can't stand following directions, so meals often develop as I go along," he said. "I guess I get some of that attitude from my uncle who was a contrarian of the first order. He was also an outdoorsman supreme; the kind of outdoorsman that only his upbringing tramping through the woods and fields of Tennessee in the 1920's could have produced."

"He taught me to use my first fly rod and showed me how to arm it with balsa poppers to lure the distrustful large mouth bass. He also taught me to cast a hand net for mullet in Tampa Bay where my grandfather had squatted and built a couple of modest cottages where our families retreated to rejuvenate body and soul each summer."
So, when Dougherty moved to New England and began exploring northeastern outdoor hunting and fishing activities, it was natural for him to cook what he caught or shot in the streams and woods.

"For many years, we went to Maine, to the Unity area for some of the best bird shooting you can imagine. "Often we'd come back to the farmhouse a friend let us crash in and cook what we bagged that day". Dougherty and a small band of upland hunters concentrated on tracking down the often maligned and frequently misunderstood woodcock, known in culinary circles as being nearly impossible to render edible.

"We would bring back a batch of woodcock and try every way imaginable to make them taste decent." Among the methods; deep frying, wrapping in bacon, drenching in various fruity concoctions. "At the end of the day", he said. "No matter how convincingly we lied to each other, they just weren't any good. It was the proverbial 'Sautee slowly in a cast iron skillet, then throw away the bird and eat the skillet'".

Then he discovered sour cream. "Where has this been all my life?"

Thus a chef was born! "If you put enough sour cream in a dish it can make anything taste good", he contends. "I've learned not to stop just with game recipes. Sour cream is great on everything from ham hocks to breakfast cereal"

After our interview Dougherty left immediately to continue wandering aimlessly through the streams and field of New England. But rather than keeping an eye out for him, watch for the release of his newest cook book ***Fixin' Yummy Stuff without Recipes".***

THE MONTANA INVITE
West Newbury, Massachusetts – December 1, 2011
Email received 6:36 pm

From: Jack
To: J.C.
Sent: Thursday, December 01, 2011 2:54 PM
Subject: Montana Fishing

J.C. I talked to Willie the other day and he thought we should consider a trip to Montana the last week of August. He tells me that it's one of the better times to find yourself knee deep in one of their historic rivers.

The Silver Forest Inn in Bozeman has accommodations with 6 or 7 bedrooms and a kitchen. We'll need to rent an SUV along with Willie's truck to get around. He tells me the fishing spots are pretty far apart but since we'll be driving at around 80 mph plus we should get us where we need to go without a problem.

Let me know if you think you can make it

Jack

From: J.C.
Sent: Thursday, December 01, 2011 3:08 PM
To: Jack
Subject: Re: Montana Fishing

Hey Jack,

I mentioned this to Sue and she quickly reminded me that our anniversary is the last week of August; the 26th to be exact and that the dog house was still open for business.

This of course immediately brought to mind the last time I tried to plan a fishing trip with you, Willie and Tim that happened to coincide with my wedding anniversary.

In case you don't recall it was the trip we planned for the fall salmon run at the Pere Marquette back in 2004 when she put her foot down and wasn't going to let me go.

I'm sure you also remember pulling into Barothy Lodge with Willie and Tim only to find me already there propped up on the screen porch enjoying a generous portion of Tennessee's loud mouth soup.

I remember your words exactly. "Jeez, JC," you said "How long you been here, and how in hell did you talk Sue into letting you go?"

"Jack", I said "I've been here since yesterday. Two days ago I was sitting in the living room watching the game when Sue came up behind me and put her hands over my eyes."

"'Guess who?', she said"

I pulled her hands off, and there she was wearing a brand new nightie. Then she took my hand and pulled me to our bedroom.

The room had candles and rose petals were strewn all over, and on the bed were handcuffs, and ropes! She told me to tie and cuff her to the bed, which of course I did.

And then she said, "Do whatever you want."

... So, here I am.

Montana in August? Already got my bags packed.

J.C

IN THE END IT'S ALL ABOUT YELLING AT SQUIRRELS
West Newbury, March 13, 2012
Wrapping it Up

As a consequence of a recent and what is apparently an inevitable onslaught of rheumatism, complimented by hair loss and expanding girth I've had to curtail my hunting and fishing activity more than I ever expected I might.

The main culprit is a rather pesky cataract that has been, along with the diminishing daylight hours of winter, causing the world to look a little more like peach fuzz every day.

All I've been able to manage for the last year or so is a hunt from the shelter of my kitchen window blind focusing on a couple of unruly local squirrels who daily engorge themselves at our bird feeder. I'm at a disadvantage as I'm armed with a twenty year old fairly anemic pellet gun.

The squirrels routinely thumb their noses at me after each encounter so that all I've really managed to do is pepper the feeder with tiny holes, many of which still retain the skeletal remains of smashed pellets.

Maybe if I'm ever successful in ending their assault on my sunflower seeds, I'll be able to use some of the squirrel recipes generously provided me by the Legendary Uncle Jim.

Unfortunately, the squirrels seem to have both the upper hand along with better eyesight for early warning. On the other hand, if I quickly open the door and yell, "Out, out damn squirrels". They immediately take off running.

It's nice to know that someone still listens to me.

Hey Bob!

The Fenway Nine kicked those Bronx Boys Butts in '04 and I've really got a good feeling about them this year!

Although the final chapter hasn't been written yet... and no fat ladies are singing at the moment, I can still distinctly hear their gentle hums in the distance.

In 2011 the Red Sox trotted out the most stupendous choke ever known to mankind, blowing a nine game wild card lead over Tampa which they had held on September 1st.

By the start of 2012 Francona and Epstein will be barely visible in the rear view mirror.

So life is in fact short for everyone...take someone fishing

Go Patriots!

For brother Bob, fisherman and companion extraordinaire!
Robert David Dougherty 1955 – 2002

15363411R00097

Made in the USA
Lexington, KY
23 May 2012